INNER MONGOLIA

CHINA INTERCONTINENTAL PRESS

图书在版编目（CIP）数据

内蒙古/内蒙古自治区政府新闻办公室编. ——北京：五洲传播出版社，2001.8
（中国西部概览丛书）
ISBN 7-80113-963-1

Ⅰ．内... Ⅱ．内... Ⅲ．内蒙古—概况—英文

中国版本图书馆 CIP 数据核字（2001）第 060049 号

《中国西部——内蒙古》编辑人员名单

编委主任： 乌云其木格
编委副主任：张国民
主   编： 孟树德、黄文聪
编   辑： 乌兰图雅、刘满贵、郁明
责任编辑： 荆孝敏
撰   稿： 黄文聪、张琛、乌兰图雅、狄瑞珍、杨宏达
摄   影： （按姓氏笔画为序）
          王景真、王金花、孔群、白国华、白斯古郎、包海山、兰红光、
          刘宝珠、刘海峰、布仁巴雅尔、宋丽君、李学君、武瑞、岳枫、
          杜梭林、和平、特木尔巴根、杨慎和、杨勇、张建生、张春环、
          张兴帮、张运成、赵树强、胡剑铭、郝继兰、郝智明、潘顺、
          斯琴、韩钢生、常子君、郭兰柱、郭义、奥静清、崔玉常、额博、
          樊明成、缪娜

封面设计： 阎志杰
版式设计： 刘鹏 刘佳景
翻   译： 李金慧

中国西部——内蒙古

五洲传播出版社
地址：中国北京北三环中路 31 号 邮编：100088 电话：82008174
网址：www.cicc.org.cn

开本：140mm*203mm 1/32 印张：6
2001 年 6 月第一版 第一次印刷 印数：1-25000
ISBN 7-80113-963-1/K·279
定价：26.00 元

Contents

Contents

Contents

WEST CHINA

Preface

$\mathcal{T}$he large-scale development of western China is called a "century project." It has captured the world's imagination because the region promises brilliant prospects for development and exceptional opportunities for business.

People are paying close attention to, exploring and studying the west. They want to know everything about it, hence the visitors, reporters and fact-finding groups heading west and the steady stream of letters and E-mails asking for information material. They are anxious because delay means lagging behind and letting a golden opportunity slip away. In order to unveil and display the western region to the world, China Intercontinental Press has compiled the Introduction to Western China Series.

Western China, with its peculiar glamour and profound historic content, has many things that need an introduction.

It is the place where the remains of the earliest primitive people in China were found. Yunnan's Yuanmou Ape Man existed 1.7 million years ago and Shaanxi's Lantian Ape Man existed 800,000 years ago.

It was the political, economic and cultural center of China prior to the 10th century. Thirteen dynasties spanning more than 1,100 years, including the Zhou, Qin, Han, Sui and Tang, established their capitals in Shaanxi.

It is an area inhabited by a large number of ethnic minorities. A total of 47 nationalities live in Xinjiang and 25 nationalities live in Yunnan. Each ethnic group has its own distinctive culture and customs.

It is China's treasure house of resources and boasts abundant resources under the ground as well as on the ground. Statistics reveal that 160 minerals have been discovered in the region. Reserves of rare metals account for more than 90 percent of the national total and hydropower reserves account for over 80 percent. Furthermore, the western region has a rich variety of biological resources and is praised as a "kingdom of plants,"a"kingdom of animals" and a "biological gene bank."

It is an important passageway leading to the outside world. The ancient Silk Road linked China with Central Asia, South Asia and Europe, and now the Eurasian Continental Bridge traverses the region. Not only a commercial passageway, western China also was the region where the Yellow River valley culture, the Ganges River valley culture, the ancient Greek culture and the Persian culture underwent exchange and integration.

It is a tourist attraction with countless scenic spots, some of which have been listed by UNESCO as world natural and cultural heritage sites.

And so on so forth. To present a complete picture of the western region, the compilers have arranged the series according to administrative divisions introducing each province, autonomous region and municipality in the region one by one. Even so, I'm afraid the presentation is incomplete.

Change in the western region is rapid, and the Chinese idiom "changes occur with each passing day" is no exaggeration when used to describe the present situation in the region. The authors of the books say their biggest headache was dealing with statistical data, especially economic figures. They made sure that every figure in the books has been treated earnestly and verified several times. However, they can't guarantee that the figures will still be true when you read the books. These figures only reflect the situation during a specific period of time. Even so, they are valuable as reference.

Since the reform and opening drive, the Chinese economy has witnessed many miracles. It is expected that more miracles will take place in the large-scale development of the western region. In a Chinese song entitled "The Story of Spring," there are lyrics that say:"The year 1979 was a spring. An old man drew a circle by the South China Sea. Miraculously, cities mushroomed and gold mountains grew." Today, western development represents another enormous circle because it covers half of the country.

The day victory is declared in western development will be the day when the entire Chinese nation takes off.

Li Bing
October 2000

Location of Inner Mongolia in China's Map

Administrative Map of Inner Mongolia Autonomous Region

Hulun Buir League
⊙ Hailar

Hinggan League
Ulanhot ⊙

Xilin Gol League
⊙ Xilin Hot

Tongliao
◎

Chifeng
◎

Alxa League

Bayan Nur League
Linhe ⊙

Ulanqab League
Jining

Baotou
◎

Wuhai
◎

Dongsheng
⊙

Hohhot
●

Ih Ju League

Alxa Left Banner
⊙

Introduction

*E*conomy of Inner Mongolia Autonomous Region has witnessed great progress since China's reform and opening-up started in 1978. Due to historical reasons and natural conditions as climate and geography, however, the region has been left far behind by eastern region, and the gap is widening. That the Chinese Government decided to carry out western

President Jiang Zemin investigated the North-Mercedes Heavy-Duty Motor Vehicle Plant on June 29, 1999

development strategy provides an unprecedented opportunity for the development of Inner Mongolia. The autonomous region must grasp the opportunity to quicken the reform and opening-up and modernization steps and try to realize the goal to lead other provinces in development at a possible early date.

Inner Mongolia plays an important role in China's western development. It is the most important ecological preventive line in north China, a resource abundant area, a front to open to the north and a gateway to safeguard the northern border.

Inner Mongolia has rich resources. The areas of grassland, farming land per capita and forest all lead the country. Of the 120 minerals found here, the proven deposit value reaches 1,300 billion yuan, accounting for over 10 percent of the country's total and ranking the third in the whole country. At present, the agricultural and husbandry production has taken certain scale. Every year it can provide 5 billion kg of commodity grains to

The luxuriant grassland of Hulun Buir has a total grassland area of 88 million hectares, accounting for one fourth of the country's total.

the state. The comprehensive production ability in this field is the best in the five pastoral areas of China. The farm and livestock products processing, especially the processing of green food, has a bright future. The deposit of coal ranks the second in the country. The conditions for turning coal into electricity has matured. The low cost and short transmission electricity line guarantee the power supply of Beijing and north and northeast China. Inner Mongolia has a unique resource of rare earth. The natural gas field found in Ordos Basin is one of the largest such fields of China. Taking the opportunity of western development and oriented by the market, the autonomous region will surely accelerate its resource transmission. This will not only help the development of Inner Mongolia, but also provide strong support to the sustainable, rapid and healthy development of the whole China.

Inner Mongolia is situated in China's northern frontier, bordering Russia and the Republic of Mongolia and spanning across the northwest, north and northeast economic zones. It is an essential part of the economy of western region. At the same time, it keeps close economic and technological cooperative relations with eastern region. Therefore, it can directly integrate into the market system of eastern and central China. In economic ties with foreign countries, Inner Mongolia has opened 18 frontier land ports including Manzhouli and Erenhot. It is known as the "bridgehead" of the "Second Eurasia Continental Bridge. " Since 1978, the autonomous region has begun opening in the north and seeking cooperation in the south, greatly promoting the frontier trade and foreign economic and technological cooperation with others. To "turn Inner Mongolia into the front for China's opening-up in north side" as proposed by Chinese President Jiang Zemin, Inner Mongolia will play a more active role in the opening-up in the future.

Inner Mongolia is the first autonomous region set up in China with the major population as minority ethnic group. Former Premier Zhou Enlai once named it a "model autonomous region. " For a long period of time, Inner

Mongolia has kept border security, national unity and political stability.

Through 50 years of economic construction, especially the work in the past 20 years, Inner Mongolia has developed into an important base of commodity grains and livestock products, energy and raw materials in north China. It is striving to become a significant energy industrial base cross the century. The industries relying on raw materials such as iron and steel, nonferrous metal, building material and chemical have a great development potential. Its aerospace, military, heavy-duty vehicles and equipment industries possess an important part in the whole country. Furthermore, the local special industries as rare earth, green food and wool textile have a broader prospect. By western development, Inner Mongolia will further bring its present advantages into full play and accelerate the structural adjustment and optimization of industries, thereby creating new favorable conditions for economic development. Now Inner Mongolia is seriously carrying out the strategy of western development. It will focus on infrastructure construction, protection and construction of ecological environment, adjustment of industrial structure, development of scientific and technological education and training of talents. In the following years, Inner Mongolia will build itself into the most important ecological defense line in north China and develop three areas of different functions. It will also finish 10 projects and three goals. The final aim is to turn Inner Mongolia into an economic growth point of China in the 21st century.

The defense line is a guaranty for the social and economic sustainable development of the region. It will not only prevent sandstorms from destroying Beijing and northwest, north and northeast China, but also fundamentally change the conditions of drought on the Yellow River and flood on the Songhua and Liaohe river valleys. If the ecological environment of Inner Mongolia doesn't improve, there will be no ecological security in Beijing and "Three Norths" belt. Without the beautiful mountains and rivers

Wind power of Inner Mongolia accounts for one third of the country's total, with an annual generating capacity of 540 million kw

in Inner Mongolia, there will be no stable life in north China. Therefore, ecological construction is the largest work in the region.

The three kinds of areas of Inner Mongolia refer to the farm and livestock and green food development zone, the energy and raw material industry development zone and rare earth scientific research and production development zone. The three kinds of areas take full use of the farm and livestock products, energy and mineral resources of the region, so they are the foundation for economic development of the region and key to the western development. They are of vital significance to the industrialization process of Inner Mongolia and establishment of advantageous pillar industry systems. Through the construction of these three kinds of development zones, Inner Mongolia is expected to realize resource transformation, industrial structure optimization and technological innovation, thereby building itself into "hometown of green food," "valley of energy" and "capital of rare earth."

The farm and livestock and green food development zone depends much on famous brands and abundant agricultural and pastoral resources. The farming land and grassland construction must be strengthened, and farm and husbandry production structure must be adjusted. While promoting the

Introduction

5

processing industry of farm and livestock products in famous brands, it will also develop the eight pillar industries: cashmere, milk, mutton and beef, leather, wheat, potato, bean and corn. It is trying to lead the country in the production and processing of cashmere, milk, mutton and beef. Recently the region will mainly carry out the following five projects: Comprehensive development of agriculture, construction of high-quality farm produce and livestock production base, development and model base establishment in pastoral areas, seedling project in agriculture and husbandry and "breeding in the north and growing in the south. "

The energy and raw material development zone will be based on the rich energy and mineral resources of the region and oriented by market. The coal-to-electricity transmission goes on and a group of large-scale power stations at coal mines will be set up. As a supplement, long-distance electricity-transmission lines will be built to quicken the steps of transmitting electricity from west to the east. Power market and high-power industry will be developed. The Wuhai High-Power Industrial Park will be set up and the Wuhai Chlorine alkali will be stressed. Besides, the gas transmission from the Ordos natural gas field in the west to the east will also be put into construction.

The rare earth scientific research and production development zone will be accelerated on the abundant rare earth resource of the region. The upper-reach industrial structure shall be optimized, the middle-reach product will be emphasized and the lower-reach product will be developed selectively. The aim is to build Baotou Rare Earth High-Tech Industrial Area into development and application center, information center and analyzing and testing center of rare earth in China.

Ten Projects:

Ecological construction. This is the primary task in implementing the strategy of western development. The project must meet the demand of sustainable development and be done on an overall and comprehensive basis. Inner Mongolia will finish seven projects in upper and middle reaches of the Yellow River, the Loess Plateau, Alxa windy and sandy area, wind erosion and sandification area in northern Yinshan Mountain, sandy area and grassland degeneration area of Horqin. They are the projects of returning farm land into forest and grassland, planting grass and stopping husbandry in pastoral area, construction of key ecological counties at the state-level, construction of "Three Norths" protective shelter, sand prevention and control, protection of the natural forest in Greater Hinggan Mountains and ecological immigration. Through these work, it plans to effectively restrain

Final assembly workshop of Baotou North-Mercedes Heavy-Duty Motor Vehicles, which was set up by introducing the complete set technology from German Mercedes Company

the deterioration of ecological environment in the autonomous region.

Transportation construction. Inner Mongolia is an important line of communications between China's east and west, so it must be developed ahead of time schedule. The road construction will focus on state and regional trunk highways, exit and major economic lines. The importance of railway construction is to open passageways for coal transportation and line to port, big and medium-sized cities and tour attractions. Besides extending the Datong-Junggar Railway, it will establish Xilin Hot-Sanggin Dalai, Jining-Zhangjiakou, Chifeng-Daban and Yirshi-Yimin railways. Meanwhile, it will expand the capacity of Jining-Tonghua and Harbin-Manzhouli railways. In civil aviation, it will mainly develop branch lines. While upgrading the existing airports, it will also set up branch airports in development zones or tourism areas such as Manzhouli and Wuhai.

Information network. Inner Mongolia will focus on the application of information network in this aspect. It will fully accelerate the informatization and network building of economy and society from a high starting point. Equipment construction in information bases will be strengthened so as to improve the coverage and usage rates and realize the mutual connection and resource share in information system. Put great efforts into the development of information industry as software development, e-commerce, database product and information service and cultivate new economic growth point. Popularize computer and network knowledge and enhance the application of information network technology in all social and economic fields. Renovate and upgrade traditional industries by information technology and try to improve the informatization level of the national economy.

Development and utilization of water resources and water-saving irrigation. Most areas in Inner Mongolia are short of water. Therefore, the development and utilization of water resources and water-saving irrigation becomes an important task. Centering on water saving, Inner Mongolia will finish the following five projects: Water conservancy pivot project, harnessing of big rivers, construction of water sources in pastoral areas, renovation of irrigation areas and drinking project of people and animals. The anti-flood projects in the trunk and branches of the Yellow River, Liaohe River and Nenjiang River will be accelerated. Water-saving projects will be conducted in the large-scale irrigation areas along the three rivers. The technology of irrigating with rain will be promoted in dry farming and pastoral areas. Greatly improve the water supply and anti-flood ability and effective usage rate of water and fully solve the drinking problem in arid areas and high-arsenic and high-fluorine areas.

Urban infrastructure construction. Inner Mongolia has few cities, which are also at small scales and with imperfect facilities. In the urban construction work of Hohhot, Baotou, Wuhai, Chifeng and Tongliao, the local government will follow the principles of "scientific planning, classified guidance, stressing key cities and gradual promotion. " The focuses will be on urban roads construction, water, heat and gas supply, sewage and garbage treatment, control of air pollution resulted from coal, garden greening and

A view of Baotou residential area.

Introduction

economical houses building. Construction of medium-sized and small cities where governmental offices of leagues are located will be strengthened. Some small towns with certain economic strength and population will be selected for major construction. Priority will be given to the construction of frontier ports and key tourism attractions. A clean, civilized and elegant urban environment will be created in cities to enhance their influences on surrounding areas.

Basic construction of education, culture and sanitation. The five projects in this area are compulsory education in poverty-stricken areas, expanding enrollment in institutions of higher learning, cross-century quality education, basic-level cultural facilities and everybody enjoying basic sanitary and health care services. Through these projects, the autonomous region tries to improve the quantity and quality of public services enjoyed by common people. By implementing compulsory education project, the special subsidy will be given to poverty-stricken areas, thus greatly improving the schooling conditions in impoverished banners and counties and laying a solid foundation for the nine-year compulsory education in the whole region. By increasing the enrollment rate in universities or colleges, Inner Mongolia will enroll more students within the region while trying to send more Inner Mongolian students to brother provinces, autonomous regions and municipalities, so as to fully improve the education quality and schooling effect. Through the cross-century project, the region will rationally adjust the school structure, improve conditions of one third middle and primary schools and shorten the distance between schools, thus creating a favorable environment for fully implementing quality education. In the basic-level cultural facilities construction, Inner Mongolia plans to set up or renovate 100 cultural stations at the township-level, 10 libraries and cultural centers each year, thus realizing the goal that each county has cultural centers and libraries and each township has cultural stations. The health care project means to launch the water-changing projects in 526 villages suffering from arsenic poison and other areas suffering from fluorine poison. The renovations will be done in hospitals in 50 impoverished banners and counties. Further strengthen the three-grade sanitary facilities in farm and herding areas, set up health care service network in urban areas and greatly improve people's health level.

Structural adjustment and industry upgrading. In this regard, breakthroughs are expected in four aspects: Development of competitive special economy, optimization and upgrading of resource industries, strategic adjustment of state-owned economy and development of non-state-owned economy. The general aim is to strengthen agriculture, upgrade industry, accelerate tertiary industry and invigorate ownership structure. The four pillar industries, i.e., farm and livestock products processing, energy industry, metallurgical industry and chemical industry, must be upgraded and renovated, and four pioneering industries: rare earth, biotechnology, information and heavy-duty vehicles, shall be cultivated. While continuing the traditional industries in fields of circulation and transportation, six new economic growth points will be explored, which are the tourism, real estate, scientific and technological service, private education, finance and insurance and community services, thus forming a new framework of the tertiary industry.

Biotechnology. Inner Mongolia boasts rich plant resources as *mahuang*, *licorice root*, *dangshen*, sallow thorn, Chinese wolfberry and desert cistanche, and animal bones and internal organs. By employing bio-pharmaceutical technology, the region can develop its traditional Chinese medicines as well as biomedicines and chemical medicines, new special-effect and health care medicines with Inner Mongolian characteristics. By employing microorganism and enzyme technology, it will develop high-class food addictives and new forage addictives. Also, Inner Mongolia leads the

Introduction

11

country in embryo transplant and artificial insemination. By promoting such techniques, Inner Mongolia intends to become the largest production base of fine breed cattle frozen semen and embryo transplant bases of meat cattle and sheep.

Grassland culture and tourism. Inner Mongolia boasts vast grassland, broad desert, exotic primitive forest, brilliant culture and strong folk flavor, so it is easy to develop tourism industry. Taking the great opportunity of western development, the tourism will become a new economic growth point of the region. The major tourism areas to be developed are Hulun Buir and Xilin Gol grasslands. Besides, centering on Mongolian, Liao Dynasty and grassland civilizations, a group of cultural projects will be finished. The construction of the Mausoleum of Genghis Khan and Wudang Monastery will go on. Desert tourism areas will also be cultivated and infrastructure construction in these areas will be perfected.

Foreign tourists visiting Mongolian yurts

Comparatively well-off standard of living. Quicken the steps on the way to a comfortable life. Various measures will be taken to improve the living and producing conditions in impoverished areas. By expanding consumption credit, the local government will lead farmers and herdsmen to increase input in house building. While properly adjusting the structure of villages, the accesses to electricity, telephone, road and TV and radio will be finished in farm and pastoral areas.

Three Great Goals.

Beautiful environment. By 2005, initial results can be achieved in ecological construction. By 2015, great results will be achieved, and by the mid 21st century, Inner Mongolia can have clean and beautiful mountains and rivers.

Stable border. Inner Mongolia will be built into a minority autonomous region featuring national unity, political stability, border security and social progress. And all ethnic groups here will achieve common prosperity.

Rich people. By 2005, the whole region is expected to realize a comfortable life. By 2015, the per capita gross domestic product (GDP) will reach or nearly reach the average level of the whole country. By the mid 21st century, Inner Mongolia will become "an important economic growth point. "

As early as in 1987, China's general designer Deng Xiaoping predicted that "Inner Mongolia might step ahead of others because of its vast land and few population. " At the beginning of 1999, President Jiang investigated the region and again proposed "to accelerate transforming resource advantages into economic advantages and strive to turn Inner Mongolia into a strongpoint in China's economic growth in the next century. " The 23 million people of Inner Mongolia are putting all out to the western development.

The Land of a Two-Hour Sunrise

WEST CHINA

Diversified Geographical Environment

*I*n north China, a long, narrow plateau stretches from northeast to southwest. This is the Inner Mongolia Autonomous Region, a beautiful and abundant land. It occupies more than 1.18 million square kilometers, accounting for one eighth of China's total territory. Of all the province-level administrative areas of China, it is the third largest one following only Xinjiang and Tibet autonomous regions.

Running along the northern stretches of China, Inner Mongolia has 3,200 kilometers of border with Mongolia and 1,000 kilometers of frontier

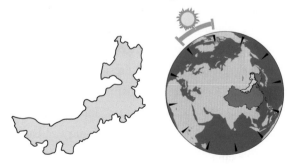

Inner Mongolia spans across 2,500 km from east to west, about one twelfth of the earth's circle. Each morning, the rising sun has to go two hours to lighten the whole region. With an area of 1.183 million square km, it accounts for one eight of the whole Chinese territory.

meeting Russia. Domestically, the autonomous region spans across the " Three Norths" (Northeast China, North China and Northwest China) and borders on eight provinces and autonomous regions. It has a total population of 23 million, made up of 49 ethnic groups, of which the Mongolians account for 3.57 million. Inner Mongolia is divided into four cities, eight leagues and two port cities, with 101 banners, counties, county-level cities and city-governed districts under their jurisdiction. The Oroqen, Ewenki and Daur are the three minority ethnic group autonomous banners. Hohhot is the capital of the autonomous region.

Situated on the famous Mongolia Plateau, most of the region lies 1,000 meters above the sea level. Highlands, mountains and plains are parallel with each other. The diversified topography includes the virgin forest on the Greater Hinggan Mountain in the east, vast desert areas around the Erdos Plateau in the west, vast fields formed by the Yellow River and Liaohe River valleys in the south, and the Hulun Buir and Xilin Gol grasslands in the north. Though situated in the arid inland area, Inner Mongolia has bountiful water resources. The fresh water in the region covers 857,000 hectares, ranking it the second most after Hubei Province in central China.

Located far from the ocean, Inner Mongolia is in the zone of continental climate. Generally cool in the summer, the region offers some escape from the heat of central China. However, during the winter, the mercury dips well below freezing point. The coldest days generally fall in January, with the monthly average temperature in the north of the region of a chilling 30 degrees below zero Celsius. Wind is frequent in spring. The sand storms, in particular, have brought many troubles and losses to the people. In the recent 30 years or so, the shelterbelts built along the "Three Norths" have helped a lot in preventing sand storms and improving environment.

Exceptional Advantages in Natural Resources

Inner Mongolia is an important resource rich area of China. On this land, there are dense forest, beautiful grassland, fertile farming land, broad water area, diversified wild animals and plants and abundant mineral resources.

The most unforgetful scene of the region is the broad grassland. *A Shepherd's Song* of the Northern Qi Dynasty (550-577) goes like this:

"By the side of the rill,

At the foot of the hill,

The grassland stretches 'neath

the firmament tranquil.

The boundless grassland lies

Beneath the boundless skies.

When the winds blow

And grass bends low,

My sheep and cattle will emerge before your eyes. "

This poem describes the beautiful scene on the vast grasslands more than 1,000 years ago. Today, the vast grassland becomes more beautiful. From the Greater Hinggan Mountains in the east to the Juyanhai Range in the west, the grassland stretches over 2,000 kilometers, covering a total area

Luxuriant herding field

of 86.667 million hectares, the largest one of China. Of them, 68.1799 hectares are usable.

On the endless greenness of Hulun Buir, Xilin Gol, Horqin, Ulanqab and Erdos grasslands, the cattle, sheep and camels attract

Diversiform-leaved poplar in autumn

many people's attention. Inner Mongolia has become one of China's most important livestock production bases. Hybrid animals such as the Sanhe horse, Sanhe cow, grassland red cow, Ujimqin fat-tailed sheep, Aohan fine-wool sheep, Erdos fine-wool sheep, Arbas cashmere goat and Alxa camel are well know in the whole China. Each year, a large amount of live sheep and cattle as well as hides and furs of the region is exported to other places of China and even abroad. The production volume of meat, sheep wool, goat cashmere, camel cashmere and milk top China. The famous products include Erdos cashmere sweater, King Deer cashmere sweater, Ili milk, Xingfa beef and mutton and green chicken.

Inner Mongolia is one of the three largest forest areas of China, ranking the second in forest area. The region boasts 350 species of trees and bushes. The primitive forests are mainly found along the northern side of the Greater Hinggan Mountains, which is called "Green Treasure House of China. " The Hinggan deciduous pine, birch and black birch growing here are of high quality. In the Hanshan, Yinshan and Helan mountains are found many secondary forests of spruce, Chinese pine, poplar and birch, which are of high economic and scientific values. The man-made forest is indispensable for Inner Mongolia. The "Three Norths" shelterbelts project launched in 1978 is reputed as "green Great Wall" and "the most significant of the world ecological projects. " Consequently, half of the farming land and most grasslands in the region are under the protection from wind.

Inner Mongolia is rich in mineral resources. To date, it has found 133 of the world's 140 proven minerals. Some 70 categories of minerals have been identified in 860 deposits around the region, including ferrous and nonferrous metals, precious and rare metals, rare earth, free elements, metallurgical raw materials, fossil fuels, chemical raw materials, building materials, and other non-metals. Of the verified mineral deposits, 41 ranks in the first five in the country in terms of volume, and six lead the nation. The deposits of iron, rare earth, niobium, zirconium and coal are vast and of high grade. In addition, they are easily exploited. The deposit of the rare earth is the largest in the world, accounting for 90 percent and 70 percent

About 800 km of the Yellow River flows through the Inner Mongolia

respectively of China's and world's total. Its coal reserves rank the second in the country. With fine conditions of turning coal into electricity, it is an ideal place to guarantee the power supply of Beijing, north and northeast

Sea of clouds in Greater Hinggan Mountain

China. The Erdos natural gas mine is the largest one found in China's land area. Most lakes in Inner Mongolia are production bases of soda, salt, mirabilite and other chemical raw materials. The region leads the country in verified deposits of soda. Deposits of mirabilite are also high. In addition, the region abounds in 30-odd non-metalic resources, such as limestone, mica,

Of the 140-odd minerals with proven deposits of the world, Inner Mongolia has found 133.

Potential value of mineral resources in Inner Mongolia hits 13,000 billion yuan

Deposit of rare earth in Inner Mongolia accounts for 90 percent of the country's total

Deposit of rare earth in Inner Mongolia accounts for 70 percent of the world's total

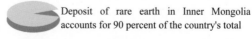

The Land of a Two-Hour Sunrise

19

vermiculite, quartz, silica sand, refractory clay, gypsum and graphite. It is estimated that the potential value of minerals in Inner Mongolia reaches 13,000 billion yuan, ranking the third in the country.

Inner Mongolia has 5.34 million hectares of fertile land, averaging 0.24 hectare pre person, which leads the country. Concentrated in the valley of the Yellow River, Tumochuan and Liaohe and Nenjiang Plains, the cultivated fields enjoy ample sunlight and abundant water, becoming the main production bases of grain and economic plants of the region. It is rich in wheat, corn, soybeans, potatoes, rice, sunflower seeds, castor beans, sugar beets and honeydew melons. The varied ecosystems of Inner Mongolia also provide good conditions for the growth of cold- and drought-resistant fruits, such as apple, pear, apricot, hawthorn and Chinese flowering crab apples.

The vast area and diversified climate of Inner Mongolia have fostered the growth of wild flora and fauna. The region is a natural treasure house of wild lives. It is home to 117 kinds of beasts, 362 species of birds and 200

Sunrise in Hulun Buir

types of domesticated or exploitable animals. Of these, 49 are under state or autonomous region protection, including 10 rare or precious animals. Such animals as the red deer, elk, reindeer, roe deer, argali, snow leopard, stoat, fox, rock pigeon, dzerin, ahu, marmot, red fox, badger, Asiatic wild ass, wild horse, wild camel, lark, swan, red-crowned crane and various kinds of wild geese, ducks and coots.

Inner Mongolia has more than 1,000 kinds of wild plants with economic value, some 600 of which are precious herbs such as Licorice root, Ephedra, Radix astragali, Skullcap root and Wolfberry. The Licorice root from the Ih Ju League and Radix astragali from Xilin Gol and Ulanqab leagues are well known both at home and abroad. Also, more than 70 fiber plants such as reed and bluish dogbane, dozens of oil-bearing plants such as hazelnut, dozens of wild fruits including hawthorn, red bean and cowberry, as well as mushroom, edible fungus and day lily are also famous.

Inner Mongolia has more than 1,000 rivers and nearly 1,000 lakes, with total surface water of 64.7 billion cubic meters. The 258 largest rivers have a drainage area of more than 200 square kilometers each. The six large water systems are the Yellow, Yongding, Luanhe, Nenjiang, Ergun and West Liao rivers. Natural lakes are scattered throughout the region. Of the 900,000 hectares of water area, 560,000 are good for cultivating agricultural products, which goes near to that of Hubei Province and 200,000 hectares more than that in Hunan Province. Both Hubei and Hunan provinces are rich in water surfaces in central China. The prospect for fresh water breeding in the region is bright. At present, the bred fish are mainly silver carp, common carp, spotted silver carp and Chinese ide. The fishing bases of Dalai, Buir (shared by China and Mongolia), Dalai Nur, Ulansuhai, Daihai and Huangqihai produce over 100 tons of fish each year.

Inner Mongolia has also rich light, wind and tourism resources. This is a land waiting to be further developed.

The Land of a Two-Hour Sunrise

21

2 The First Minority Autonomous Region of China

Remote Civilization

*T*he long history of the ethnic minority groups inhabiting Inner Mongolia constitutes an important part of Chinese culture. The remains of the Dayao Culture, unearthed in the east suburb of Hohhot, can be traced back 700,000 years. The area was a large stone processing site during the Paleolithic Age. The discovery of Hetao Man, who lived in the present regions of Uxin Banner of Ih Ju League 50,000-35,000 years ago, has

rivaled the discovery of Upper Cave Man in Zhoukoudian outside Beijing.

The Hongshan Culture, dating back to 5,000-6,000 years and characterized by painted pottery, polished stone and jadeware, was discovered in Chifeng City. Yinshan Mountain is China's largest treasure house of cliff paintings. Scattering along a mountain range

Cliff paintings in Mandula Mountain of Alxa League

stretching from Guyang County to Alxa League, the cliff paintings capture a wide range of subjects. Among these are wild and domesticated animals, hunting scenes, tribal battles, important historical events, ceremonial dances, astrological symbols, footprints, the Sun God, phallic symbols, and other abstract representations.

The creation of the cliff paintings began during the Late Paleolithic Era, and continued during the Neolithic, Bronze, and early Iron ages. Some additions were made during the Ming and Qing dynasties (1368-1911). The paintings display the social development of the ancient ethnic groups in north China. Further evidence of early human civilization can be found in the relics of the Xinglongwa and Xiajiadian cultures of Chifeng city, the Zhukaigou Culture in Ih Ju League, the Laohushan (Tiger Mountain) Culture in Ulanqab League, the Gaxian Cave Ruins in Hulun Buir League, the Ulanqab and Alxa cliff paintings, and the Erdos bronzewares.

Birthplace of Northern Chinese Ethnic Groups

Inner Mongolia is the cradle of many ethnic groups in north China,

Gaxian Cave--birth place of Xianbei ethnic group

which witnessed frequent exchanges between these nomadic tribes and the Han in the Central Plains. Such nationalities as Xiongnu, Tujue, Dangxiang, Qidan, Nuzhen, Mongol and Han once lived here.

During the Warring States Period (BC403-221), Inner Mongolia saw the construction of segments of the Great Wall by Qin, Zhao and Yan states. At the end of the 3rd century BC, the Xiongnu set up the first slavery regime on the Mongolian Plateau, controlling the whole plateau and vast territories to its west. During the heyday of the Xiongnu regime, the Qin and Han

Heicheng Ruins-an ancient city in the Western Xia Dynasty

dynasties (BC221-220AD) controlled the Central Plains. War and peace alternately dominated relations between these two mighty factions. In the end, the Xiongnu accepted vassal status under the Han Dynasty. The Tomb of Wang Zhaojun in the south suburb of Hohhot is said to be the burial place of a concubine of Emperor Yuandi of the Western Han Dynasty (BC206-25AD), who was married to the king of the Xiongnu as a guarantor of peace and friendship.

During the waning years of the Han Dynasty, the Xianbei rebelled in the east of today's Hulun Buir League. They overthrew the Xiongnu and drove their rebellion into the Central Plains, founding the Northern Wei Dynasty (386-534). The Xianbei is seen by modern Chinese historians as the first legitimate minority region in central China.

During the 100 years spanning the mid-6th and mid-7th centuries, the Tujue regime was established and immediately came into conflict with the Sui and Tang dynasties of the Central Plains. The period has seen intense warfare.

In 907, the Qidan subjugated the other northern ethnic groups and founded a dynasty, whose name was transformed into Liao in 947. The Song Dynasty (960-1279) eventually rose from the ashes of earlier central Chinese dyansties and confronted the Liao. The 74-meter-high brick pagoda, called "Daming Pagoda", standing in Ningcheng County of Chifeng City today, was said to be built during the Liao Dynasty.

As the Northern Song Dynasty began the long journey into decline, the Nuzhen rose up in northeast China. They conquered the Liao Dynasty and founded the Kin Dynasty (1115-1234), continuing the confrontation with the Northern Song Dynasty and the Southern Song Dynasty.

During the 12th century, the Mongol nomads wandering along the Erguna River in the Hulun Buir Grasslands began to consolidate and grow in strength. Early in the 13th century, Genghis Khan unified the tribes living on the Mongolian Plateau. Over the following years, Genghis Khan and his successors waged a series of wars against the Kin and Southern Song dynasties and finally unified the country and established the Yuan Dynasty (1271-1386).

Hometown of Genghis Khan

Genghis Khan (1162-1227) was born in a Mongol aristocratic family. It was a time when all aristocrats on the Mongolian Plateau fought for

Tomb of Wang Zhaojun

property and slaves. When he was nine, his father was poisoned to death by one of his enemies.

In 1189, he was elected head of Qiyan aristocratic league of Mongols. Using his intelligence and bravery and by defeating others one by one, Genghis Khan united all ethnic groups on the Mongolian Plateau and dominated a vast land from Alta Mountain in the west to the Hinggan Mountains in the east. In 1206 when he was 34, he set up the Great Mongol regime.

Once he ascended the throne, he started reforming old systems of Mongol. He launched a new military system under which he divided the whole people into 95 units, each with 1,000 persons. Under such unit is 100-person unit and under 100-person unit is 10-person unit. Each 1,000-person unit is given a fixed place to herd and corvee and soldiers are employed on such unit. At the same time, he also unified the language of Mongol. Genghis Khan included nearly 100 tribes on the grassland in his Great Mongol, thus forming the Mongolian nationality.

After the unification, the increasing thirst for wealth of Mongolian aristocrats and declining of neighboring countries provided to Genghis Khan a good opportunity to plunder outside the Mongolian Plateau. After completing the system establishment in Mongol, he put all his efforts into the wars conquering foreign lands. Using the contradictions between different nations in the Central Plains, he overthrew Xia and Kin, ending the separatist rule since the Tang Dynasty and laying a solid foundation for his successors in setting up the Yuan Dynasty. The west expedition of Genghis Khan brought great disasters to Central Asia, but it broke through the borders of Asian and European countries and promoted the economic and cultural exchanges between east and west.

Liberation of Ethnic Groups From Japanese Invaders

After China's defeat in the Opium War of 1840, the major powers of the day, including Russia, Japan, Britain and the United States, took turns to invade Inner Mongolia. In the wake of the Sino-Japanese War (1894-95), the area came under the spheres of influence of imperial Japan and Russia.

As the reign of the Qing Dynasty came to a close, the Western imperialist powers demanded reparations from China. The Qing rulers carried out new policies in Inner Mongolia aiming at raising capital. These policies included opening the borders, arranging immigration to reclaim and cultivate wastelands, setting up banks and post offices, building factories and railways, enforcing a legal and judicial system, and building schools and cultural facilities. In addition, government officials and private businessmen were allowed to join foreign investment in the industrial mining sectors.

These innovations, to a certain degree, stimulated the development of the economy in Inner Mongolia, but failed to eradicate the basic role of feudalism. More deeply involved in the semi-colonial and semi-feudal activities of the Qing Society, all nationalities in the region joined in the patriotic fight against imperialism, feudalism, and the Qing Dynasty's reclamation and cultivation of wasteland.

During the Northern Warlords Period (1912-27), the Japanese imperialists plotted the establishment of puppet regimes under the guise of independence for the Mongol and Man peoples. Local people united to resist these usurpations of power.

It was not until the birth of the Communist Party of China (CPC) that the people of Inner Mongolia took their first step on the road to national liberation. At the start of the 1920s, a group of revolutionary youths, including Duo Songnian, Lu Yuzhi, Ulanhu, Kui Bi and Ji Yatai, studied at a school for Tibetans and Mongols in Beijing. These youths organized the revolution in Inner Mongolia.

In 1926, under the direction of the CPC, the resistance movement exploded in Duguilong. In 1927, events at Guhuntan shocked the areas beyond the Great Wall. The mass revolution against feudalist privileges and the oppression of the Northern Warlords was so vehement that it enhanced the further development of the revolution of the Mongols.

In 1929, Ulanhu, who later served as vice president of the People's Republic of China, returned to Inner Mongolia from the Soviet Union to lead the fight. Faced with the Japanese presence at Hohhot and Baotou, the Communist Party established the Mongol-Han Anti-Japanese Guerrilla Force. This force worked together with the Daqingshan Detachment of the Eighth Route Army. They boldly made their way to Daqingshan Mountain and fought against the Japanese invaders in the surrounding areas. At the same time, the Northeast Anti-Japanese Allied Forces were also entering Inner Mongolia and engaging the Japanese army from its flank.

In 1945, the main force of the Eighth Route Army began operations based in Inner Mongolia. On August 15 that year, the Japanese emperors declared an unconditional surrender. Led by the CPC, the people in the region at last defeated the Japanese invaders and liberated their homeland from the humiliating reign of the Japanese aggressors.

Local heroes immediately threw themselves into the struggle for Liberation War (1945-49) and the movement for autonomous rule. As a result of the continuous, hard struggles of these revolutionary forerunners, the Inner Mongolia Autonomous Region was formally established on May 1, 1947.

Autonomous Policy

The Inner Mongolia Autonomous Region was the first minority autonomous region in China. The founding of autonomous governments reflects a mingling of ethnic groups, regional differences, politics and economies. The People's Congress and its Standing Committee and the people's government of the Inner Mongolia Autonomous Region form the administrative organs of the region. They act on their own to administer local politics, economies, finance, culture and education.

The deputies to the regional People's Congress are selected according to

Yinhe (Silver River) Square of Baotou-Capital of Rare Earth

the present and historical conditions of structure of minority ethnic groups in the region. This guarantees representation for the Mongols and other ethnic minorities. The ratios of Mongols and other ethnic groups in congress surpass their actual rations in population. Government departments at all levels employ as many ethnic minority officials as possible. Again, their actual proportions in office at all levels of government far exceed their respective proportions in the total population.

The CPC Committee of the Inner Mongolia Autonomous Region and the local government pay great attention to the development and use of minority languages. Mongolian is used in all social activities. Mongolian and Chinese are both used at meetings attended by Mongols and other ethnic groups who don't understand Chinese, but speak the Mongolian language. Both Mongolian and Chinese are equally recognized as official languages of the region. The regional government encourages cadres of the Han working in minority areas to learn the Mongolian language, and also encourages the

Ceremony to celebrate the 50th anniversary of the founding of the Inner Mongolia Autonomous Region

Mongols to learn Chinese as a second language.

After the founding of the Inner Mongolia Autonomous Region, the local government set up autonomous prefectures in the areas where other ethnic groups lived in compact communities. In the 1950s, three such prefectures at the county level, the Oroqen, Ewenki and Daur autonomous banners were set up. Later, an additional 15 autonomous townships were established.

People's governments at all levels of Inner Mongolia Autonomous Region have strictly implemented the regional autonomy policy of CPC and brought great historical changes to the region.

Nationalities in Inner Mongolia

The vast lands of Inner Mongolia are home to substantial population of 49 ethnic groups, including Mongol, Han, Man and Hui. They live together in harmony and mutual understanding.

Each ethnic group has its own history and brilliant culture. They have unique language, character, religious belief and folk customs of their own. Now the Mongolian, Han, Hui, Man and Korean languages are used in the region. People here believe in Buddhism, Lamaism, Islam, Catholicism or Christianity. Due to differences in historical environment and natural and geological conditions, ethnic groups carry out different economic activities and follow different life styles and folk customs. Inner Mongolia is like a colorful nationality museum, providing to people rich experiences.

Historical Changes

Great changes have taken place in the economy and society of Inner Mongolia since the reform and opening-up more than 20 years ago. Agriculture and husbandry have seen harvests in consecutive years; industry and enterprises enhance their strengths and production is increasing steadily; new framework has been formed in opening-up and living standards of both urban and rural people is improving daily. The Inner Mongolia today is an important base of not only forestry and husbandry, but also energy, raw

Per capita GDP in 1999 was 5,362 yuan

The total financial income was 14.375 billion yuan, a 9.5 percent increase over the previous year

materials, grain, oil and sugar. It is exerting an increasingly greater influence in economic areas of northeast, north and northwest China and playing a bigger and bigger role in the whole development framework of the nation.

Living standards of urban and rural people improve conspicuously. In 1999, the Inner Mongolia Autonomous Region completed a gross domestic product (GDP) of 127.1 billion yuan and the per capital GDP was 5,362 yuan, ranking the 16th in China and the 2nd in western regions. The total financial income was 14.375 billion yuan, a 9.5 percent increase over the previous year, which was higher than the average level of the country.

The steady development of the national economy has brought great changes to people's living standards. Food and clothes problems have been basically solved, and Inner Mongolian people have full confidence to achieve higher goals. In 1999, the per capita disposable income of urban residents was 4,770 yuan, ranking the 22nd in China, and the per capita average income of farmers and herdsmen was 2,003 yuan, ranking the 18th of the country. The increase in income has fundamentally changed people's consumption concept. People care more about nutrition in food, elegance in clothes, high quality of goods and wide space in living. Both urban and rural residents live in wider spaces, and house decoration has become a hot issue. Most families turn their eyes to telephone, air conditioner, personal computer, automobile and tourism.

Rich harvests in agriculture and husbandry for years running.

Husbandry is a pillar of Inner Mongolian economy, but its development is restricted by traditional way of production. In 1947, the amount of livestock was less than 7.8 million. After the household responsibility system was carried out in both grassland and animals, a "green revolution" has swept across northern part of the region. Raising animals while building grassland replaced the traditional extensive husbandry. Since 1985, the region has seen harvests in husbandry. In 1999, the total amount of domesticated animals reached 74.36 million, leading the whole country. Major livestock products increase sharply, of which wool, cashmere, camel cashmere and milk have been leading the China. Each year, Inner Mongolia provides 12 million livestock and hundreds of thousands of tons of animal skin, wool and cashmere to the country.

Hetao Plain in the Bayan Nur League and Tongliao City are the two largest commodity grain bases of China. From 1979 to 1998, the production volume was increasing at an annual rate of 7.3 percent, faster than the average level, i.e. 5 percent, of the whole country. In 1999, Inner Mongolia was hit by great disasters, but it still got a harvest. The total output volume of grain that year was 14.285 billion kg and the volume possessed by each person was 605 kg, ranking the third place in China. Also, the per capital possession of oil and beetroot topped the country. The fruits

Grain possessed by each person was 605 kg, the third largest in China

The total grain output in 1999 was 14.285 billion kg

and melons produced here, including watermelons, sweet melons of Hetao Plain, grapes, apple-like pears of Hetao and Red Star brand apples of Ih Ju League, all have their own characteristics. Most agricultural and livestock products here are non-polluted. Many kinds of grains are beneficial to health care. Inner Mongolia provide 3 billion kg of commodity grains to the country each year.

State-owned enterprises' reform deepened and industry vitality strengthened. When the autonomous region was founded, it had few industries and enterprises. The industrial basis was very weak. Through 50 years of construction, especially practices of reform and opening-up in the recent 20 years, the region has formed four pillar industries: the processing industry based on livestock products, the energy industry based on coal power, the metallurgical industry on iron and steel and machinery and electronics on heavy-duty vehicles. Such brands as Erdos, King Deer, Shiqi, Ili and Xingfa enjoy high reputations in the whole country.

Industrial added value in 1999, 44.227 billion

Industrial added value in 1998, 39.942 billion

In 1998, the industrial added value of the region was 39.942 billion yuan, 344 times that in 1947. The figure rose to 44.227 billion yuan in 1999. The industrial products of Inner Mongolia saw their position advanced continuously. Now, the electricity

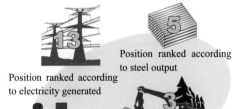

Position ranked according to electricity generated

Position ranked according to steel output

Position ranked according to timber output

Position ranked according to crude iron output

it generated is the 13th most in China, the output of pig iron is ranked the 10th, that of steel, the 5th and that of timber, the 3rd. At present, 18 enterprises from Inner Mongolia are listed on the stock market. They are: Inner Mongolia Huadian, Erdos B, Ili Share, Fulong Thermal Power, National Group, Inner Mongolia Hongfeng, Natural Alkali, Caoyuan (Grassland) Xingfa, Mingtian (Tomorrow) Science and Technology, Ili Coal B, Rare Earth High-Tech, Ningcheng Laojiao, Huazi Industry, Jinyu Group, Shiqi Industry, North Share, Yili Group and Xishui Share.

Social courses flourishing. At present, the Inner Mongolia Autonomous Region possesses 500,000 professional technicians, nearly 140,000 persons with senior or medium technical qualifications, 324 scientific research institutions and a large number of experts and scholars having great influences in both home and abroad.

The amount of livestock in 1947 was 7.8 million

Inner Mongolia has also formed a complete educational system. It has 18 universities and colleges, enrolling 49,700 students, and 106 technical secondary schools, enrolling 101,000 students. The enrollment rate of school-age students has reached 99.44 percent, and that of junior middle schools is 96.6 percent. The nine-year compulsory education has been popularized among 58.31 percent of its population. Priority is given to education of minority ethnic groups. The adult education and vocational education develop rapidly.

The medical care and sanitation

The amount of livestock in 1999 reached 74.3616 million

- 108 libraries
- 104 cultural centers
- 1,611 cultural stations
- 13 art galleries

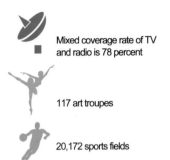

Mixed coverage rate of TV and radio is 78 percent

117 art troupes

20,172 sports fields

conditions also improve greatly. A health care network has been basically formed covering both urban and rural areas and sanitary service capacity is strengthened. Each 1,000 persons have access to 2.67 hospital beds and 2.4 doctors. Medicine work of Mongols was inherited and developed, with the only Mongolian medicine preparation center set up in Hohhot with investment from the state.

Culture and sports also thrive. Now, the region has 108 libraries, 104 cultural centers, 1,611 cultural stations and 13 art centers for the masses. Besides, it has 117 artistic performing troupes. The mixed coverage rate of radio and TV broadcasting reaches 78 percent. Sports are popular among common people. Inner Mongolia can now provide 20,172 fields for sports at different levels. Of all the people, 33.05 percent often participate in sports and exercises. This is nearly the same with the national average level.

per 1,000 persons

possess 2.4 doctors and 2.67 hospital beds

Building Ecological Shelter in North China

The Most Important Ecological Shelter in North China

*S*panning across northwest, northeast and north China, Inner Mongolia Autonomous Region composes the most important ecological shelter in these parts of China. Within the border of the region, the Yellow River flows through nearly 1,000 km. Also, it is sources of several other water systems. The northwest wind from Siberia first goes across the Inner Mongolia before it meets the warm and humid southeast wind. Therefore, it is a major factor influencing the climate of east Asia.

Inner Mongolia is the wind mouth of China. The ecological conditions here play a big role in the environment of north China. It is essential not only to the protection of environment in Beijing and Tianjin, but also to the establishment of a beautiful northwest China.

Each year, the region will see 20-80 days of great wind. The number of windy days in its northwest reaches over 55, while some goes up to 87. Since the Mongolian Plateau is formed on the rising of the Mediterranean Sea, plus the strong wind and water erosion, many stone pieces, sand and yellow earth have been brought out. Each spring, it becomes the source of sandstorms in north China.

The high plains in north Inner Mongolia are the largest natural grassland of China. They are where Mongolian ancestors lived a nomadic life and conducted husbandry work, and regarded a green shelter in north China. On the founding of the People's Republic of China, husbandry industry develops quickly and the amount of livestock multiplies. For a time, the grassland was overloaded, resulting in degradation. The sandificated area accounted for 40 percent of the total. The decline in grass quality and quantity becomes a major factor preventing the further development of husbandry and weakened the protective function of the grassland as a ecological shelter.

The Greater Hinggan Mountains in the northeast is the largest coniferous forest in north China. It is the conservation area of the sources of Nenjiang and Songhua rivers and acts as a shelter to Songhua and Nenjiang River Plains. However, in the past 50 years, the amount of timber cut has far exceeded that of timber growth. As a result, the forest resources are sharply reduced and water conservation function declined, which led to floods in the Nenjiang River.

The branches of the Nenjiang River in East Inner Mongolia, the West Liaohe River Valley in its southeast and northern side of Yinshan Mountain and Ordos Plateau in its south are where agriculture meet husbandry in north China. The complicated landscape, fragile ecological system, increasing population and over-cultivation in the past have led to serious land regeneration and water and soil erosion, which further resulted in poverty of local residents.

The Alxa Plateau in west Inner Mongolia boasts many ancient animal and plant species and is therefore called a "gene treasure house" of China. The famous two-humped camel grows here. The Ejina River oasis to the west of Alxa Plateau, the segment sacsaoul forest and the forest and vegetation in Helan Mountain are three natural shelterbelts for ecological environment. In recent years, water consumption of the Heihe River in upper and middle reaches of the Ejina River becomes more and more, greatly reducing the water volume in Ejina River. Consequently, the diversiform-leaved poplar and red willow woods disappeared. What's more, the sacsaoul forest is also declining. These led to more frequent and stronger sandstorms in Alxa area and its neighboring areas and even to Beijing.

Entering the 1990s, sandstorms occur more and more frequently. The Juyan Sea, with a water area of 300 square km, dried up in 1992. People could no longer see such a blue space on the map. The low mountain areas bordering Shanxi, Shaanxi and Inner Mongolia, due to its severe soil and water erosion, is included in international list of such conditions. The sandificated area on the north side of Yinshan Mountain and the desert and semi-desert area in west Xilin Gol League and north Ulanqab and Bayan Nur leagues are suffering from shortage of both surface and underground water and degenerated grassland. The sandificated area in Mu Us and Hunshan Dake deserts is enlarging. Part of Hetao and West Liaohe river saw salinization. Hulun Buir, though with large precipitation and fine land, also faces danger of desertification because of its thin level of earth.

Desert oasis

39

If an ecological shelter can be built in the region, the dry northwest wind will slow down its speed and China's north drought and south flood condition can be changed. Inner Mongolia is a key area to be protected for its bio-diversity. Each grass is a soldier in the region. When they are united, they form a formidable troop. Surface water in Inner Mongolia mostly comes from mountain forest and the water conservation ability in wetland is five times that of forest. Therefore, it is a great ecological project to plant trees and grass in Inner Mongolia and launch wind and sand prevention and water conservation projects, thereby improving the environment of north China as well as Beijing. However, all work must be done on the real conditions of the region and following the natural and economic rules. With people's unremitting efforts, the Inner Mongolia can be built into a place with ever-green mountains and rivers.

"Green Great Wall" Under Construction

To protect ecology and prevent sandification, all ethnic groups in Inner

Each year, the region plants trees on a land of 700 hectares

Afforestation to prevent sands

Mongolia put out all their efforts. Since the reform and opening-up in 1978, especially in recent years, the region has given much priority to the protection and construction of ecological environment. It is trying to plant more trees and add greenness to the region. Of the 10 forestry ecological projects determined in the 1970s, five are in the Inner Mongolia. They are the "Three Norths" protective shelterbelts construction, sand prevention and harnessing project, landscape engineering in plains, protective forest construction in the middle reach of the Yellow River and protective forest construction in the Liaohe River Valley.

Inner Mongolia takes up nearly one third of the tasks in the "Three Norths" project, the most one in the 13 provinces and autonomous regions involved. It also carries on 40 percent of sand prevention project, and 52.6 percent of Liaohe River shelterbelts work. In the natural forest protection project and state ecological county construction project started in 1998, Inner Mongolia also takes up a big proportion. In the natural forest protection project launched in 2000, 29 banners or counties, including Alxa, Bayan Nur, Ih Ju and Wuhai of the region, are included.

The "Three Norths" Protective Forest is the largest ecological project in the world. It was launched in 1978 and will be completed by 2050. The whole project covers 551 counties (banners, cities or prefectures) of 13 provinces and autonomous regions of northeast, north and northwest China, with an area of 4.06 million square km. The planned forest area is 35.08 million hectares. Upon completion, the forest coverage rate will increase from the 5 percent in 1975 to 14 percent. Eighty-six banners and counties of Inner Mongolia are in the project list, with a total task of 10.80 million hectares to be finished.

In the first phase project of the "Three Norths" (1978-1985), Inner Mongolia set up 181,300 hectares of forest, 2.4 percent more than the schedule, thus increasing the forest coverage rate from 4.7 percent to 7.6 percent. During the second phase (1986-1995), the region finished the

Since 1981, the region has closed 28.962 million hectares of hillsides to facilitate afforestation

plantation on an area of 2.7526 million hectares, of which 2.0333 million hectares are man-made forest and 90,500 hectares are planted by aerial seeding. Besides, there are 638,700 hectares of mountains are closed for vegetation. The third phase goes from 1996 to 2000. In this period, Inner Mongolia will finish a vegetation task of 1.15 million hectares, among which 833,000 hectares will be man-made forest, 83,300 hectares aerial sowing forest and another 233,300 hectares be closed for planting trees. The work goes on smoothly.

The vegetation under control in model areas has improved from 5 percent o 40 percent

In the east of Inner Mongolia, there is a sea of forest covering over 100,000 square km. This is the largest state-owned forest-Greater Hinggan Mountains. It is nearly of the same size with the Jordan of Asia or Iceland of Europe, housing over 7,200 wild animals and plants. The total timber deposit, mainly larch and white birch, reaches 670 million cubic meters. Therefore, it is called a "green treasure house. " Yakeshi, a city at the foot of Greater Hinggan Mountains, is closely related with forestry industry. Every day, tens of thousands of timbers are transported to other places of China. Other timber products, such as fiberboard, shaving board, veneer board, high-quality floor board and tannin extract can all be found here. Since the natural forest protective work started in 1995, Inner Mongolia has grown

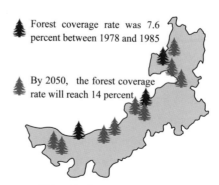

Forest coverage rate was 7.6 percent between 1978 and 1985

By 2050, the forest coverage rate will reach 14 percent

"Three Norths" protective shelter

Building Ecological Shelter in North China

43

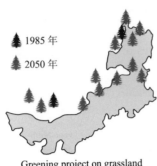

▲ 1985 年

▲ 2050 年

Greening project on grassland

1.1333 million hectares of forest, and a favorable circulation including wood-cutting, processing and renovating has been formed.

The Engebei Ecological Comprehensive Development Model Area in west Inner Mongolia has a total area of 150,000 hectares. It is all covered with deserted land. To its west and south is the Hobq Desert, which accounts for 80 percent of the development area.

Hobq Desert is one of the largest deserts of China, which divides Hetao Plain from Ordos Plateau. As a belt, it spans across the Ih Ju League. It has a total area of 16,500 square km, about 19 percent of the league. Engebei faces the Yellow River in the north, so the mountain flood becomes a fierce natural disaster for it. In flood seasons, the gullies in middle and east Hobq will swallow large areas of farmland and villages and cause break-up in transportation. What's more, the water flow eastward intensifies the damage in middle and lower reaches of the Yellow River. By July 1989 when the Engebei model area was set up, there had almost been no residents on the land.

In November 1991, the Hobq Desert Comprehensive Development Model Zone was set up in Ih Ju and harnessing of Engebei started. Yuanshan Zhengying, professor of Japanese Niaoqu University and chairman of Desert Plantation Practices Association, started planting trees in Hobq in 1990 after he investigated Engebei. He vowed he would devote all his life to the harnessing of Engebei and would bury himself there upon his death. His action has inspired tens of thousands of Japanese and Chinese. They set up organization to support the Engebei project. Yuanshan has been advocating an industrial way of developing desert and believed there must be considerable profits in the future. Meanwhile, officials, workers, students and other common people all join the great campaign.

In 1998, Engebei was listed as a key ecological project of the state and also a key project in national agricultural comprehensive development. In the past 10 years, a lot of projects have been carried out in Engebei, including the large scale wind-prevention and sand fixation project; trees plantation along the desert road, green passageway along the two sides of the north exit, vegetation in lake area, protective forest in farmland, economic forest, seedling and herding grass seeds project and flood diversion project. Through these work, a comprehensive protective forest system has basically taken the shape and plays a bigger and bigger role in ecological environment.

To date, 2.5 million arbors have been planted in the model area, 85 percent of which survived. Also, there are over 3 million bushes such as salix mongolica and 666.7 hectares of land are cultivated by diverting water from flood. Such economic plants as licorice root and gourd are grown on

Wetland ecological nature reserve in Hulun Lake

45

an area of 66.7 hectares and high-quality grass on 670 hectares. Besides, there are two grape fields, covering an area of 5.3 hectares and a garden covering 6.67 hectares. A 16.7-hectare seedling base majoring in cuttage of Xinjiang Poplar and setting of a kind of pine and a 20-hectare grass seed base mainly compose of alfalfa and sweet clover have also been formed. Nearly 10,000 hectares of land have been harnessed and 5,300 hectares of grazing land been restored. The vegetation coverage rate in the controlled area has increased from the previous 5 percent to present 40 percent. At the same

1780 元

2000 年

1994 年

The net income of farmers and herdsmen doubled that in 1994

time, a dam extending for dozens of km was built up in the area, forming a green shelter from south to north. Edible plants such as licorice root and common sow thistle growing in flood detention basins surrounded by trees have become popular food in the market. The improved ecological environment has drawn many birds back.

Since 1995, the Ulanqab League has carried out a new strategy. That is once one mu of high-yield land is cultivated, two *mu* of erosion land will be returned to grow trees and grass. People of the league call the agricultural ecological project "the second innovation" to compare it with the first one in the 1980s when household responsibility system was promoted in rural areas. In this way, farmers and herdsmen in this area are expected to bid farewell to traditional agriculture.

For years, the Ulanqab League has put in 25 million yuan in ecological project. Officials of the league give 30 percent of their salaries each month to support the work of returning farmland into forest and grassland.

The ecological project here is called a "government project. " By 1999, the league had dug 14,000 motor-pumped wells and 20,562 tube-shaped wells. The irrigated area has increased by 60,480 hectares. The film covered corn for the first time settled down in the league, with 133,300 hectares. The growing area of potatoes also grew from 100,000 hectares in 1994 to 266,700 hectares. The area of irrigated

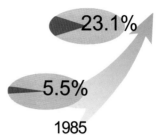

Forest coverage rate has improved from 5.5 percent in 1985 to the present 23.1 percent

and non-irrigated high-yield farming land rose to 466,700 hectares. To put it in another word, one third of the sowing land here produced two thirds of grains. Meanwhile, the league has planted 533,300 hectares of trees and grass, and basic effect can be seen in 200,000 of them. About 29,980 hectares of protective forest was set up, which can protect 400,000 hectares of farming land. The 426,700 hectares of barren hills, slopes and little river valleys have been harnessed, and the forest coverage rate was raised to 7.5 percent. The cross-county ecological project in Wuqi County on the north side of Yinshan Mountain is 300 km from east to west and 50 km from north to south. The rates of heads of livestock going to slaughterhouses and going to market are respectively 47.2 percent and 36.3 percent.

Given the condition that farming land was reduced by one third, the grain output of the league keeps the steady at 1.2 billion kg for three consecutive years. The husbandry industry grows at an annual increase rate of 7 percent rather than the 2 percent before. The total amount of livestock reaches 6.33 million and net income of farmers and herdsmen is 1,780 yuan, double that of 1994. The ecological development in big stride has laid a solid foundation for the economic development and overall poverty alleviation of the Ulanqab League. It has decided four leading industries: the potato, grain other than wheat and rice, meat and animal skin products. The refined starch processing industry in the Qahar Right Wing Front Banner is one of the four industries of the same kind with an annual production ability of 3,000 tons. The high quality and great output volume of potato have drawn an investment of 335 million yuan from US Sunlight Food Co., Ltd, Taiwan Sanda Food Co., Fuguang Company of Hohhot and Nailun Group. As the Shuanghui Group of Henan Province joins, the beef and mutton processing industry flourishes. The league is capable of processing 3 million frozen cows and sheep each year, and can process 1.2 million animal skins and 50 million hide products. The rough and refined processing plants have covered every corner of the league, and 190,000 farmers and herdsmen go to the market. Of their net income, 70 percent comes from processing industries.

Daqinggou-a state-level nature reserve

After 20 years of efforts, Inner Mongolia has seen great progress in ecological construction, especially in forest building. Through the plain vegetation project carried out in 20 banners and counties since 1986, more than 65 percent of farming land has been under protection of forest, and the forest coverage rate has increased from 5.5 percent in 1985 to the present 23.1 percent. In the sand prevention and harnessing project starting in 1991, 2.131 million hectares of land have been harnessed. The protective forest projects in Liaohe River Valley and middle reach of the Yellow River, the comprehensive harnessing of water and soil erosion in upper and middle reaches of the Yellow River and ecological harnessing project in the sandy area of the Loess Plateau all go on smoothly. Besides, Inner Mongolia also launched the "green passageway" projects along the Beijing-Baotou and Baotou-Lanzhou railways and the No. 110 state highway, the Daqingshan forest construction project and village vegetation project.

The quality of forest building is increasing annually. In recent years, it can finish 333,300 hectares of man-made forest, 66,700 hectares of aerial sowing, 66,700 hectares of hill closing and 40 million trees planting each year. In 1999, it was hit be severe drought, but the forestry tasks were all finished. Its work in forest building and vegetation has been awarded many times by the state. Of the 42 banners and counties accomplishing over 1 million mu of man-made forest, 21 are from Inner Mongolia. Now a "green Great Wall" is emerging on the vast land, and shows great ecological, social and economic profits. Now, 1.7667 million hectares of farming land and 2.1333 million hectares of grazing land have been included in the protection of forest, 24 percent of water and soil erosion area controlled and 20 percent of sandy area harnessed. A pleasant picture with dense forest, abundant grain, rich grass and livestock arises.

Forever Greenness in Mountains and Rivers

Inner Mongolia Autonomous Region needs 50 years to totally change its ecological environment. It has to call on people of different ethnic groups, rely on science and technology, enhance protection of existent natural forest and wild animals and plants, plant trees and grass in a large scale, harness water and soil erosion, prevent desertification, build ecological agriculture, improve people's living and working standards, strengthen comprehensive governance and complete a group of projects influential to the national ecological environment. It plans to launch such projects as returning farmland to grassland and forest, planting grass in grazing land and stopping herding, key ecological county setting up, protective forest of the "Three Norths", sand prevention and harnessing, protecting natural forest in the Greater Hinggan Mountains and ecological migration in the upper and middle reaches of the Yellow River, the Loess Plateau, the sandy area of Alxa, sandificated area of northern Yinshan Mountain, Horqin area and degenerated grassland. Through these efforts, it plans to improve the ecological environment of the region.

In vast grazing land, the top task of ecological environment construction is to restrict grassland degeneration and establish a husbandry system combining industrialization and intensification. Fine land (about 10-15 percent of the total) must be selected to grow grass and used to set up artificial grassland and fodder bases of various kinds and different classes, and

Man-made forest

Deer and tourists are in harmony in the central square of Baotou

regional seed basis should also be set up. Field for grass cutting must be cultivated and properly utilized and fodder processing and storage system by set up to improve the raising conditions of livestock in winter. Rotation grazing will be promoted and herding conditions in warm seasons should also be improved. In this way, a sustainable development featuring economic, environmental and social profits can be expected in grassland husbandry.

Great efforts should be put in harnessing water and soil erosion in juncture of agriculture and herding areas and Loess Plateau hilly areas. The harnessing project will center on little river valleys, plus such biological measures as tree and grass planting, vegetation construction and rotation of grass and grain and engineers of building dams and cultivating farmland. This should become a key project in the middle reach of the Yellow River, Nenjiang River Valley and upper reach of the West Liaohe River.

Active measures must be taken to control sandstorms in Horqin, Hunshan Dake, Mu Us, Hobq, Ulanbuhe and Tengger deserts. By setting up arbor forest and bushes at the same time and using ways of aerial sowing and man-made planting, various kinds of wind prevention and sand fixation net should be formed.   A composite way of operation combining agriculture, husbandry and forest is encouraged.   In sandy areas with a humidity index over 0.3,   a cow raising model can be set up and artificial grassland can be cultivated on beaches among sand hills.   In the area where irrigation is available,   an optimized model can be employed.   Vegetation should be restored on floating sands by aerial sowing.   In dealing with desert,   the border area and area with relatively favorable conditions should be particularly treated so as to set up man-made oases of different forms and scales.   Sand control experiences in Inner Mongolia can be used as good examples for such work in other places.

Meanwhile,   sand control work should be stressed in Beijing and Tianjin municipalities.

In May 2000,   Premier Zhu Rongji led relevant ministerial and department officials to carry out an on-the-spot investigation in Duolun County,   Zhenglan and Taipusi banners in the southern border of Hunshan Dake Desert.   He gave out important guidelines to the sand control work in Inner Mongolia,   especially that in Beijing and Tianjin.   Also,   he decided to set up a leading group of ecological environment construction in the

A pearl on grassland-Xilin Hot

region, which is composed of the State Forestry Administration, State Development and Planning Commission, Ministry of Agriculture, State Environment Protection Administration and Ministry of Water Resources. The group will provide guidance to the sand prevention and control work and help solve real difficulties and problems in ecological construction.

The three sandy areas surrounding Beijing and Tianjin to be specially harnessed are Hunshan Dake, Horqin and northern side of Yinshan Mountain, involving 53 banners and counties. The tasks recently are as follows: First, draw out plans, perfect policies, implement tasks and launch the masses and start the harnessing as soon as possible. The Inner Mongolia Autonomous Region has set up a leading group, under which are corresponding institutions. They will coordinate and guide the ecological construction work within their own spheres. Second, carry out a responsibility system with both work divisions and coordination. All relevant departments should give their due support to sand control work. Officials and technicians must go to the sandy area themselves to provide to basic workers technological guidance and engineering supervision. Also, media including newspaper, magazine, film, TV and radio should be fully used to publicize the significance of the sand control work and introduce good examples in such work, thereby forming a favorable atmosphere in improving ecological environment. Third, increase input through multiple channels. The region should give priority to ecological protection projects in arranging funds. Financial departments should try to overcome difficulties and simplify procedures in making small-loan credits, giving their support to ecological construction and livestock sheds building. The policy must be properly carried out that the one works will benefit. By aerial sowing, hill closing, man-made forest and protective shelter building, the bad influences of sand sources to Beijing and Tianjin can be expected to reduce.

Building Ecological Shelter in North China

4   Building an Economic Development Platform for the New Century

*T*ransportation, posts and telecommunications and urban construction are important basis and essential conditions for the development of national economy. Also, they are major fields for western development of China. Through 50 years of construction, Inner Mongolia has built up a broad platform for economic take-off and overall social progress in the new century.

Transportation Network Extending in All Directions

The beautiful, rich and broad Inner Mongolia Autonomous Region, starting from Greater Hinggan Mountains in the east and ending in Juyanhai in the west, spans across 4,000 km in northeast, north and northwest China and goes through 3,000 km from north to south. It borders Russia and Mongolia. The unique geographical position has decided its strategic significance in economy, politics and security. The state has paid much attention to the transportation construction in the region. Since the PRC was founded in 1949, especially after the 20 years of reform and opening-up, Inner Mongolia has seen great strides forward in transportation. A system with railways, roads and civil airs has linked it to all other parts of China.

Railway. At present, there are 14 state-owned trunk railways, 12 state-owned feeder railways and 5 locally-owned railways, with a total operation mileage of over 125,000 km. Two of the railways lead to foreign countries. One is the Harbin-Manzhouli Railway, which meets with Siberia Railway of Russia after the Manzhouli; the other is Jining-Erenhot, which extends to Mongolia. These are important passageways linking China and Europe. Main domestic trunk lines include Beijing-Baotou, Baotou-Lanzhou, Jining-Tongliao, Tongliao-Huolinhe, Baotou-Shenfu and Fengzhen-Junggar railways. Among them, the Baotou-Lanzhou Railway gets onto the track of Xinjiang railway and then connects the Eurasia Continental Bridge, thus forming a third passageway between China and Europe. The Beijing-Baotou Railway meets Datong-Fenglingdu and Datong-Qinhuangdao railways in the east and Lanzhou-Urumqi Railway in the west. It is a trunk line linking inland China with sea ports. The Beijing-Tongliao Railway is connected with northeast railways in Tongliao and Beijing-Baotou Railway in the west, acting as a tie of northeast, north and northwest

Hailar Airport

Hohhot-Baotou Expressway

China. The 943-km-long Jining-Tongliao Railway is the longest local railway in China. It covers four leagues and cities and 13 banners and counties of the region and started operation on December 1, 1995. The railways can link Inner Mongolia with Manzhouli, Beijing, Shanghai, Xi'an and Lanzhou.

In the first decade of the 21st century, Inner Mongolia will strengthen its efforts in building railways to the sea. It will expand the railway scale and set up border railways with political, economic and defense significance. The major projects are: First, complete the construction of Sanggin Dalai-Zhangjiakou, Chifeng-Daban, Yimin-Yirshi, Wuhai-Dongsheng railways, which are connected with Tianjin, Jinzhou, Tumenjiang (Hunchun) and Huanghua ports. Second, expand the transport capacity of Jining-Tongliao Railway and bring its role to full play. Third, accelerate the renovation of such railway pivots as Jining and Baotou by improving technology standards and build Jining-Zhangjiakou Railway to shorten the time from Beijing to Baotou. Fourth, while making the two international railways more convenient, build the Linhe-Hami trunk railway. It will be another railway to foreign countries.

Road. The road mileage of Inner Mongolia has exceeded 63,800 km. Road is available in 95.5 percent of all its townships. The major projects finished in the past 20 years include Xilin Hot-Baochang-Zhangjiakou, Hula,

Wulanhua-Saihantala, Yakeshi-Manzhouli, Hohhot-Laoyemiao, Tongliao-Ulanhot, Jingpeng-Xilin Hot roads and ring road of Baotou and Linhe. In 1997, the Hohhot-Baotou Expressway was completed. It is the first expressway of the region. Since then, communication between Hohhot, Baotou and Ih Ju, where one half of Inner Mongolia's industrial fixed asset and two thirds of scientific and technological strengths accumulate, becomes more convenient. The second phase of Hohhot-Baotou Expressway, with a planned length of 151 km and budget of 1.5 billion yuan, started in July 2000. This is the first infrastructure construction project in the western development strategy of the region, an important part of No. 110 state expressway, an easy way to link northwest China and Beijing and eastern ports and a passage between Hohhot-Baotou economic zone and industrial corridor.

What's more surprising is the 100-km-long road in the Hobq Desert. Like a dragon, it sits in the middle of the desert, on both sides of which trees and grass have formed a green corridor. Under fierce conditions and facing the capital shortage, 130,000 people of Hangjin Banner put all out to finish and keep the road.

In the first 10 years of the 21st century, Inner Mongolia will accelerate the construction of state highways and trunk roads as well as regional great passageways for western development, take an active part in defense and border roads, perfect the road net in the region and try to improve the quantity and quality of roads going to townships and administrative villages.

The construction will focus on the following: First, complete the Laoyemiao-Hohhot-Baotou-Linhe-Wuhai section of the No. 110 state expressway (the Laoyemiao-Baotou section will be finished by 2005), thereby creating a great passageway linking China's west, northwest and north China, Beijing and Tianjin. By then, the time cost from Hohhot to Beijing will reduce from the present 6-7 hours to 4-5 hours. Second, develop a regional road passageway, which will be composed of part of expressway

Highway bridge on the Yellow River linking Baotou and Dongsheng. Now Inner Mongolia has five road or railway bridges set up across the Yellow River

and first- and second- class highways. The passageway, starting from Manzhouli and through Hailar, Ulanhot, Tongliao, Chifeng, Jining, Hohhot, Dongsheng, will arrive in Yinchuan, capital of Ningxia Hui Autonomous Region. The passageway will span across the northeast, north and northwest China. Besides, passageways from Erenhot through Baotou to Beihai and from Ejin Banner through Yinchuan to Wuhan will also be built. Third, perfect the local road network by finishing 11 local trunk roads including the one from Alxa Right Banner to Ejin Banner. Fourth, build 12 roads between banners and counties including the one from Tu Right Banner to Liangcheng. Fifth, accompanying the poverty relief project, build roads to townships and administrative villages. The aim is to make roads available in all administrative villages.

Civil Aviation. For years, Inner Mongolia has been strengthening the construction of airports and improving their comprehensive guarantee ability. Since 1985, it has carried out large-scale renovation, expansion and resettlement of seven big airports within the region. Now the Hohhot Airport has come up to the 4D standard, which can meet the demand for the taking off and landing of Boeing 767. Baotou and Hailar

Road mileage

airports are of the 4C standard, which are available for Boeing 737 to take off and land. And airports in Chifeng, Tongliao, Xilin Hot and Ulanhot are at the 3C standards, which can meet the demands of BAe146. There are flights to Beijing every day in Hohhot and Baotou. The time needed between Beijing and Hohhot is only 45 minutes.

Equipment and facilities in telecommunication, navigator and weather forecasting which are advanced in the world in the 1990s have been put into use, and airport construction has also developed. The Baita Airport in Hohhot has been approved by the State Council as a port of aviation and acclaimed by the International Civil Aviation Organization one of the 14 international routine flights in China. The Dongshan Airport of Hailar was also restored to a port of aviation with the approval of the State Council, which becomes a new window for opening up of Inner Mongolia.

By 1999, the region's seven airports had possessed 19 domestic air routes and one international route flying to 17 cities home and abroad. Many domestic and foreign airlines came to invest here. In 1998, Hohhot began chartered cargo flights to Russia. This becomes a new economic growth point of the region. To date, Inner Mongolia Civil Aviation has signed international or national contracts for sales of passenger and cargo services with Air China, China Eastern Airlines and China Southern Airline, thus forming a computer

Telecommunication building of Hohhot

sales net covering the whole region.

In the first decade of the 21st century, Inner Mongolia plans to develop several branch agencies for tourism and economic development based on its only conditions while improving the present airport facilities. It will continue the perfection of Hohhot Airport, bring into full play the trunk airlines in central and west China, update Xilin Hot and Tongliao airports, resettle Chifeng Airport and build Wuhai and Manzhouli airports and Bayan Hot, Huolinhe and Arxan simple airports to meet the demand of civil aviation and agriculture and husbandry.

Post and Telecommunications Change Quickly

With the coming of information age and network age, post and telecommunications have become an essential part of people's life. By fully employing advanced science and technology, post and telecommunications have developed rapidly in the region and greatly promoted its social and economic progress.

Postal Service. Through years of construction, postal services in Inner Mongolia have made great progress. Now a modern post network going through railway, road and aviation and covering the whole region, connecting the whole country and even the world has been set up. By the end of 1999, the total fixed capital in postal services had reached 1.5 billion yuan. The whole length of lines for postal services was 62,000 km. All townships and towns have access to post and offices at or above the banner or county level have realized computer operation. Eight express postal routes have been opened between Hohhot and Beijing and express letters can reach every corner of the world.

Postal services in Inner Mongolia do not stay only on letter, package, remittance and publication issuance, but also extend to fields of commodity, information and currency. The businesses can be categorized into the following three aspects: First, postal or mail delivery. Besides the traditional businesses of letter, package, express letter, publication issuance and confidential communication, Inner Mongolia has opened a large number of new businesses, including commercial letter, gift sending, mail order, advertising, newspaper and magazine retailing and wholesale of audio and video products. Second, financial business such as deposit and remittance of residents. Also, taking advantages of its network and high-quality services, postal departments at all levels have developed such services as receiving

Herding people also use mobile phones

telephone, water, electricity and coal gas fees, delivering wages, pensions for the aged and opening insurance accounts. Third, electronics and information businesses. By relying on comprehensive postal computer network and modern communication ways, post offices at different levels have launched e-commerce, e-mail and mixed mail services. While opening new businesses, postal departments of Inner Mongolia have also realized professional operation in postal deposit, publications issuance, gift sending, postal order and advertisement. In this way, the operation mechanism becomes more smooth and operators' enthusiasm is aroused.

Telecommunications. Backed by advanced science and technology, the telecommunication network in Inner Mongolia has quickly transferred from artificial, automatic and analogue stages to digital network. This is a historical step forward. At present, a secure and reliable telecommunication net characterized by rich content, high speed and digitalization, which is centered on optical cable communication and supplemented by satellite and digital microwave communications, has been formed. It covers the whole region and is connected with all China. The telecommunication industry has developed from a "bottleneck" which restricts the social and economic development to a pioneering industry in promoting social progress and economic development. The first-class long-distance cable line at the state

level Beijing-Hohhot-Yinchuan-Lanzhou and other cable lines at the provincial level such as Hohhot-Xi'an, Hohhot-Beihai and Zhalantun-Qiqihar, Ulanhot-Baicheng and Chifeng-Chaoyang have linked up all Inner Mongolia.

The nomadic tribe now lives in buildings

Small-scale machine brings clean water to animals

The technological equipment also improves greatly. The SDH technology advanced in the world has been applied to most transmission equipment. Now the public phone network is capable of installing 2 million telephones and over 1.5 million families have installed telephones. Cell photos have become popular in herdsmen on the grassland.

The multi-media communication and information services also develop rapidly. The video conference, multi-media long-distance digit and distance medical care are widely used. Promoted by the government network, many enterprises and families also realize work through computer network. The improvement of telecommunications has greatly optimized the investment environment of the region, accelerated its process of capital invitation in China and opening-up in the world and exerted far-reaching influences to the social and economic development of Inner Mongolia.

In the first 10 years of the 21st century, Inner Mongolia will go on strengthening the construction of telecommunication lines and postal pivots in big and medium-sized cities. Meanwhile, it will improve the post and

Building an Economic Development Platform for the New Century

A new town-Xuejiawan

telecommunication services in townships and administrative villages. By digital ways such as cable, wireless and satellite transmission, it aims at expanding its digital communication scale and improving communication quality and speed. Also, it will actively introduce optical cable to buildings and living quarters and experiment with family wide bands by using ATM switches. Mobile communication, data communication, multi-media communication and intelligence network will also be developed to meet the demands of social and economic development.

Daily Perfecting Urban Infrastructure Construction

Urban infrastructure construction is the basis of a city. By scientific planning and strict implementation of the plans, Inner Mongolia has successfully mingled historical, cultural and ethnic characteristics with the present age in its urban construction, achieving a great harmony in building and environment. Since 1978, with the growing of its economic strength, the region's urban construction step also quickens. It has conducted many large projects including water, gas and heat supply as well as garbage and sewage treatment facilities.

Hohhot, capital and political, economic and cultural center of Inner

Mongolia Autonomous Region, and a famous historical and cultural city of China, covers an area of over 17,000 square km, with a population of 2.04 million. The urban area is 780,000 square km, with a population of 710,000. In 1995, it was entitled a "model city of the country in comprehensive harnessing of urban environment. "

Through years of efforts, Hohhot has taken on a new look and its overall function has improved a lot. This can be shown in the following aspects:

Water supply. Using the money raised through multiple channels, the local government strengthened the construction of water plants. Now, the comprehensive water supply capacity of the city has reached 242,000 cubic meters per day. The project of diverting the water from the Yellow River with a loan from Japan started in August 1998, which will meet the demand of Hohhot for water in the future.

Public transport. The municipal government gives much priority to public transport in improving its transportation conditions. Now, each 10,000 persons possess five public transport vehicles. Meanwhile, the government imposes strict restrictions to the taxies for they have made up great pressure on roads.

Gas supply. To save energy, reduce pollution, protect environment and improve people's living standard, the municipal government is increasing the supply of coke oven coal mine and liquefied petroleum gas. Now most houses have used clean gas.

Heat supply. The municipal government of Hohhot is enhancing its ability of supplying heat in a concentrated way. It expands the area of central heating and joins thermal and power plants. New small-scale boiler houses are forbidden to be set up. Now 45.6 percent of households in the city enjoy services of central heating. The second-stage project of central heating, with a designed ability of 5.1 million square meters, started in 1998, which, upon completion, will greatly improve the heat supply capacity of Hohhot.

Building an Economic Development Platform for the New Century

Roads and bridges. Since 1996, Hohhot has built and renovated a group of roads and bridges. It renovated 25 roads and built a new urban flyover. Also, two flyovers for railways were also set up.

Drainage works. At present, 80 percent of the city area have been equipped with drainage pipelines. Sewage treatment plants have been expanded and the sewage handling capacity for the first-class and second-class ones are respectively 150,000 tons/day and 100,000 tons/day.

Environment and sanitation. The city accelerates the construction of garbage stations. The garbage collecting and transporting are done in a close way. The rate of garbage transport in living quarters is 100 percent.

Urban vegetation. After professional tree plantation and voluntary planting of all the people, a green framework at a certain scale has been formed. Now the public green area possessed by each person is six square meters and the vegetation coverage rate is 27 percent.

Baotou, the largest city of Inner Mongolia, has also made conspicuous achievements in urban construction, especially in the construction of square, green land, roads and buildings.

In future, Inner Mongolia will grasp the opportunity that the state is carrying out the policy of urbanization and plan its urban construction in a scientific way, thereby promoting the urbanization process in the region. It will put more efforts in the construction of Hohhot and Baotou, give support to medium-sized and small cities where league and city governments are located, select small towns where banner and county governments are located and choose some border ports and tour cities. By 2005, it plans to improve the urbanization rate of the region to 40 percent.

The urban construction will focus on improving environment and enhance functions of a city. The aim is to build Hohhot into a modern capital city and turn Baotou into a regional center featuring prosperous economy, beautiful environment, civilization and cleanness and having influences on

Floating market on the grassland

surrounding areas. In medium-sized and small towns, construction will focus on roads and public transport, water and heat supply system, sewage and garbage treatment, garden vegetation and economical houses. In developing townships, the autonomous region will pay much attention to turning population-intensive area into industry-intensive area and combining township construction with the transferring of surplus labor forces, development of tertiary industry, promotion of husbandry and improvement of townships. In this way, these townships may become important carriers of the secondary and tertiary industries in agricultural and herding areas.

Major Social & Economic Indexes of Inner Mongolia From 1978 to 1999 (Table 1)

Items	Unit	1978	1980	1985	1990	1995	1998	1999
I. Population								
Total population at the end of the year	10,000 persons	1823.0	1876.50	2015.90	2162.55	2284.38	2344.88	2361.92
II. Employment								
Number of employees at the end of the year	10,000 persons	652.80	698.37	856.63	924.55	1029.40	1050.30	1056.68
III. GNP	100 million yuan	58.04	68.40	163.83	319.19	832.77	1192.19	1270.94
IV. Investment in Fixed Assets								
Total investment in fixed assets	100 million yuan	16.56	15.21	52.42	70.77	273.06	350.16	383.0
Investment in fixed assets by state-owned institutions	100 million yuan	13.91	14.97	37.77	56.77	210.00	225.69	244.52
Capital construction investment	100 million yuan	13.91	13.12	27.40	39.72	136.92	168.73	195.11
V. Finance								
Financial income	100 million yuan	6.90	4.13	13.39	32.98	76.35	131.23	143.75
Financial expenditure	100 million yuan	18.69	18.37	36.27	60.90	102.18	181.76	212.47
VI. Price Index (With the price last year as 100)								
General retail price index of commodities			101.0	105.5	108.5	102.9	116.80	98.1	97.7
Price index of residents' consumption			101.5	106.1	108.9	101.8	117.50	99.3	99.8
Price index of agricultural products and sideline products			101.3	112.0	113.5	95.2	124.70	97.3	93.8
VII. People's Life								
Disposable income of urban residents	Yuan	301.01	407.13	676.64	1155.00	2845.72	4353.02	4770.53
Per capita net income of farmers and herdsmen	Yuan	131.37	192.37	399.62	647.45	1300.00	1981.48	2003.00
Per capita net income of farmers	Yuan	126.07	181.35	360.41	607.15	1208.38	1911.12	1903.00
Per capita net income of herdsmen	Yuan	188.00	265.18	649.86	905.67	1870.97	2515.98	2698.00
VIII. Agriculture and Husbandry								
1. Added value of agriculture, forestry, husbandry and fishery	100 million yuan	18.96	18.03	53.54	112.57	260.18	341.62	331.24
2. Output of major agricultural and livestock products								
Grain	10,000 tons	499.00	396.36	604.10	972.97	1055.40	1575.4	1428.27
Oilseed	10,000 tons	12.50	25.00	79.50	69.38	70.2	90.3	100.89
Licorice root	10,000 tons	43.10	81.16	254.17	236.44	263.5	259.2	136.78
Forest area built	10,000 hectares	29.79	29.81	70.41	29.75	40.25	47.78	53.40
Pork, beef and mutton	10,000 tons	20.89	23.80	34.93	50.10	73.95	117.89	129.74
Milk product	10,000 tons	7.24	7.03	25.86	39.65	51.17	67.11	71.20
Wool	10,000 tons		4.06	5.08	6.15	5.99	6.93	6.94
Cashmere	Ton		1803	1362	2076	3114	3876	3825
Aquatic product	10,000 tons	1.50	1.14	1.79	3.04	4.76	6.20	6.86
3. Total amount of livestock at the end of the year	10,000	3586.50	3753.24	3667.31	4254.35	4795.04	5206.3	5147.56
Draught animal	10,000	659.30	681.26	736.58	707.47	708.26	677.3	667.39
Sheep	10,000	2378.10	2553.39	2468.38	3023.93	3321.04	3712.9	3702.62
Pig	10,000	549.10	518.59	462.35	522.95	765.74	816.1	777.55

Note: The indexes of the magnitude of value in the table are all based on prices of the year.

Major Social & Economic Indexes of Inner Mongolia From 1978 to 1999 (Continued)

Items	Unit	1978	1980	1985	1990	1995	1998	1999
IX. Industry								
1. Total Industrial Added Value	100 million yuan	21.84	27.30	45.90	87.18	254.88	399.42	442.27
2. Output of major industrial products								
Raw coal	10,000 tons	2194.00	2210.98	3203.86	4761.61	7055.21	7769.48	7070.93
Crude salt	10,000 tons	65.18	43.00	66.34	93.28	76.13	148.28	132.07
Timber	10,000 cubic meters	378.17	414.55	502.07	525.96	504.35	486.86	379.23
Electric power	100 million kwh	37.78	49.05	80.46	169.54	278.54	350.41	380.61
Sugar (including crude sugar)	10,000 tons	4.23	6.92	17.88	16.37	17.07	20.12	11.95
Dairy product	10,000 tons	0.31	0.42	1.43	2.20	3.03	3.76	5.42
Knittingwool	Ton	2464	3905	4726	4349	4925	1357	1826
Woolen fabric	10,000 meters	336.80	337.31	806.75	1041.85	1477	414.73	279.10
Machine-made paper and paper plate	10,000 tons	4.25	4.24	9.53	13.59	19.15	13.76	14.27
Cement	10,000 tons	91.91	109.85	185.11	227.97	349.27	486.82	549.70
Steel	10,000 tons	99.00	133.04	170.47	273.01	355.36	404.37	416.30
Pigiron	10,000 tons	107.00	137.63	182.37	280.66	345.78	408.74	424.86
TV set	10,000 sets	0.10	1.38	17.51	38.45	32.68	3.42	12.54
X. Transport and Post and Telecommunications								
Volume of cargo circular flow	100 million ton km	224.55	174.92	442.51	621.90	785.12	844.35	1005.8
Railway	100 million ton km	214.96	164.78	424.30	519.41	625.56	657.08	805.1
Road	100 million ton km	9.59	10.14	18.20	102.49	159.56	187.27	179.7
Volume of passenger circular flow	100 million passenger-km	31.80	43.19	82.52	99.01	173.58	187.91	206.7
Railway	100 million passenger-km	22.38	31.84	58.34	57.54	71.97	76.13	89.2
Road	100 million passenger-km	9.42	11.35	23.86	38.07	89.85	100.44	108.2
Post and telecommunications	10,000 yuan	4159	4547	6348	11729	96552	247762	356740
XI. Wholesale and Retail Trade								
Total retailing volume of social consumption goods	100 million yuan	31.01	34.18	75.64	130.58	295.02	400.89	437.38
XII. Foreign Trade								
Total export volume of foreign trade	US$10,000	1026	2663	13708	32456	60840	82343	90600
Total import volume of foreign trade	US$10,000	526	1735	4740	15974	51470	56238	70200
XIII. Culture, Education and Health Care								
Number of students in universities and colleges		12126	17405	31242	32428	37248	43553	49732
Number of students in secondary technical schools		24927	35775	40184	49800	57656	81479	101400
Number of students in middle schools	10,000	106.07	135.54	111.66	106.62	109.35	117.90	122.2
Number of students in primary schools	10,000	291.78	289.86	254.90	234.29	234.31	224.84	213.68
Kinds of newspapers published	10,000			16353	16107	16286	16495	17605
Kinds of magazines published	10,000		580	1853	1264	1036	1484	1562
Number of health care institutions		4000	4350	4749	5160	4915	4641	4468
Beds in hospitals		25023	49630	53572	60727	66515	65794	66361
Number of health workers		59277	70022	87130	96734	102187	104890	101312

Note: The total volume of purchasing, selling and storing commodities in 1998 refers to the wholesale and retail trade with a sales volume of over 5 million yuan.

5   Kingdom of Green Food

$\mathcal{I}$nner Mongolia has exceptionally advantageous natural conditions in producing green food.   The quantity and quality of green products here lead the country.   This is a new economic growth point.   In the process of western development,   it will bring more potentials into play.

Rich Green Resources

Inner Mongolia has a vast area,   broad grassland,   fertile farming land and exuberant forest. The rich resources create a fine ecological environment for the development of green products in this region.

Compared with those of some developed countries and other places of China,   the air,   water,   soil and plants of Inner Mongolia are less polluted and less destroyed.   It is a "holy land" rarely seen in developing green industries.   According to experts,   most of the 101 banners and counties of Inner Mongolia are suitable to the development of green products.   In the region,   333,300 hectares of land are under environment supervision as raw material sources for green products and 4.5333 million hectares are under environment supervision as grassland.   Also,   Inner Mongolia spans across a broad area, with sufficient sunlight and varied living beings. These are all premises for the development of green products.

Advantages in developing non-polluted livestock products. Of the whole area of Inner Mongolia, 60 percent are grassland, covering from Hulun Buir in the north to the Erdos in the southwest and Horqin in the east and Alxa in the west, which accounts for one fourth of the country's total. On the six great grasslands, which are Hunlun Buir, Xilin Gol, Horqin, Ulanqab, Erdos and Urad, grow over 1,000 forage plants, one tenth of which are of high value, including sheep grass, icy grass, brome grass without awn, wild rye, alfalfa, wild pea and wild axle grass. The fertile grassland cultivates abundant livestock, including Sanhe horse, Sanhe cow, grassland red cattle, Ujimqin fat-tailed sheep, Ohan fine-wool sheep, Inner Mongolia fine-wool sheep, Erdos fine-wool sheep, Arbas white goats and Alxa camel. They provide rich non-polluted raw materials for the development of wool textile, dairy products, fur and leather industries.

Hongshan Reservoir. The region has now 29 reservoirs of different sizes.

Kingdom of Green Food

Advantages in developing non-polluted agricultural products. Inner Mongolia possesses 8.2 million hectares of farming land, with 0.36 hectare to each person, four times that of the national average. The major agricultural area is found in the eastern and southern part of Greater Hinggan Mountains and Yinshan Mountains, Hetao Plain, Tumochuan Plain, West Liaohe River Plain, Plain at the west bank of Nenjiang River and vast hilly land. With varied soils as black earth, chernozem and chestnut soil and usable ground and underground water resources, they have become a grain storehouse of China. Inner Mongolia, sitting in the northern border of China, has a long winter and little precipitation. However, because of the varied topographies, climate, little pollution, sufficient sunlight and great temperature difference between day and night, most areas can realize one harvest one year. Also, there are rains in warm days. These compose favorable conditions for agricultural production. Now four rational agricultural production areas have been formed, which are the high-quality wheat production area of Hetao and

The Yalu River with the Greater Hinggan Mountains. Inner Mongolia boasts 109 rivers with an annual flow of over 20 million cubic meters

Tumochuan plains, high-quality corn production area of West Liaohe River Valley, high-quality bean production area in the southeast of Greater Hinggan Mountains and high-quality potato production area in central and western

Autumn scene of Greater Hinggan Mountains

area of the Inner Mongolia. Some other agricultural produce bases have also been selected and some high quality and profitable economic plants bases including those for Hetao sweet melons, late-maturing watermelon, apple-shaped pear, red pepper, green-house vegetable, tobacco and traditional Chinese medicine have taken shape.

Advantages in developing non-polluted wild plants. Inner Mongolia boasts rich plant resources. In Greater Hinggan Mountains alone, there can be found 2,300 varieties of wild plants, of which over 500 are natural medicinal plants. As science and technology progresses, most poisonous plants such as langdu, horse-drunken grass and bitter bean has been developed into precious medicinal plants. Wild economic plants include oak nut, hazelnut, mushroom, edible fungus, daily lily, *facai*, brake fern, reed, Siberian cocklebur, bitter apricot kernel, cowberry and dusi.

Green Products Enjoying Reputation Home and Abroad

To meet the demand of the market, Inner Mongolia has put great efforts in developing green products. In the whole region, there are now 78 enterprises engaged in green products and 176 products are using the mark of

Kingdom of Green Food

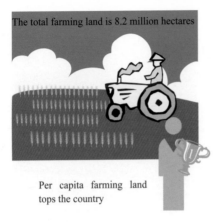

The total farming land is 8.2 million hectares

Per capita farming land tops the country

80 percent of the world's cashmere comes from Inner Mongolia

green food. The total volume of green food hits 500,000 tons, the most in China.

Cashmere products. Inner Mongolia contributes 80 percent of the cashmere of the whole world. The white goat cashmere produced here, which is "white as snow, light as cloud and soft as silk", has got the reputations of "fiber diamond" and " soft gold" in the world market. It has won for many times the International Cashmere Award held in Italy and Golden Award of China Agriculture Fair. In recent years, its cashmere industry develops quickly. Now, there are over 140 cashmere processing industries or enterprises in the region, 59 of which has an annual production ability of 12,000 tons. The Erdos Group Company and King Deer Cashmere (Group) Company have become famous both at home and abroad. The KVSS cashmere produced by Erdos Group is called "No.1 cashmere of China". The Erdos cashmere sweater won high-quality titles 14 times in the autonomous region, six times from the Ministry of Light Industry and two times from the state. It is approved as "China Famous Product" and "Chinese Consumers' Satisfactory Product" by China Product Quality Association, and possesses the largest market share in the same trade. The King Deer cashmere products has also won the "Golden Award of China International Famous Products Fair" and such titles as "China famous brand" and "Chinese Consumers'

Satisfactory Product." The cloth it produced has won the "International Golden Horse Award" and "International Golden Award for High-quality and Fine Product" endowed by the Spanish Government. Its domestic market is enlarging and international market has also developed from Japan and Hong Kong Administrative Region to dozens of other countries and regions. Inner Mongolia enjoys a good reputation in the quantity and variety of cashmere products, fashion of cashmere clothes and sales market.

Dairy products. Inner Mongolia is an important base of milk products. Of the cow milk, sheep milk, camel milk and horse milk, the cow milk, with a total output of 670,000 tons, is the most, accounting for 90 percent of all the milk. The dairy product processing industry started in the 1950s. By 1998, it had developed 109 enterprises. The daily milk processing ability is 2,400 tons and the annual ability is 720,000 tons. In the 1980s, the dairy products developed from several species to dozens of species, and a group of new products and high-quality ones were produced, including mother milk-like milk powder, fast-dissolving whole milk powder with sugar, high-protein milk powder, sour-addicted fungus milk powder, icecream milk powder,

Kingdom of Green Food

Relic gull

Mongolian gazelle

There are over 110 precious and endangered species of wild animals in the region, including swan

Roe deer

solid juice-taste milk, milk tea powder, sour-addicted fungus bean powder, milk powder and cheese for longevity, sour milk, condensed milk, milk cake and milk with bacteria-free package. Of them all, the fast-dissolving milk powder has the largest output. Ili Group Company, the largest dairy producer in the autonomous region, has been listed among the top three enterprises of the same kind after 15 years of development. Its ice cream and Lile bag milk has the largest production volume in China. The sales network of these products covers the whole China and some neighboring countries including Russia, Mongolia and Viet Nam.

Grain and oil products. The wheat produced in Hetao and Tumochuan plains has a relatively higher index in protein, gluten and subsidence rate, so it is superior to other wheat species of China. The flour made of it is of high quality and greatly welcomed by consumers. It sells well both at home and abroad. The Hetao snow-white flour and Dagong series flour have been appraised as famous brand of the autonomous region and won the golden award of the Second China Agriculture Fair. Inner Mongolia has now nine flour production lines advanced in the world, with an annual production ability of 540,000 tons, of which the Liangfeng of Bayan Nur and Dagong of Inner Mongolia are the best. Besides, Inner Mongolia is abundant in sunflower seeds and rape seeds, a great source for oil production. In Bayan Nnur League alone, the oil output volume per year hits 50,000 tons. The yearly output of Golden Deer brand refined oil in Baotou reaches 30,000 tons.

Meat products. Inner Mongolia is the largest production base of non-polluted livestock products. The mutton and beef enjoy good reputation in China and foreign countries. The Donglaishun Instant-Boiled Mutton Restaurant, with a long history in Beijing, is using the mutton from Sonid Grassland. Each year, a large amount of mutton and beef sell to Russia and

The rape field is waiting for harvest

Wild day lily. The region has altogether over 1.500 kinds of precious plants

other countries of the Commonwealth of Independent States as well as Japan, middle east areas and Hong Kong SAR of China. In China's mainland, the mutton and beef are mainly supplied to Beijing, Tianjin and Northeast provinces.

At present, the meat products of Inner Mongolia include processed fresh and frozen animal meat, fresh and frozen bird meat and animal meat products. However, the processed meat accounts for only 7.5 percent of all the meat products of the region. Most export products are live animals. Therefore, the meat processing industry has a great potential.

The meat processing industry has taken the lead in industrialization. For example, the Chifeng Xingfa Group can produce 30,000 tons of chicken meat each year, with an annual sales income of 343 million yuan. By crosswise alliance, the Shandong Jinluo Group joined hands with Tongliao Meat Processing Plant, forming the Tongliao Jinluo Meat Product Co., Ltd., which can produce 96,000 tons of ham and slaughter 300,000 pigs and 100,000 cattle each year. The local industry of raising pig and cattle has been promoted. The Shuanghui Group of Henan Province, after merging the No.1 and No.2 meat processing plants of Jining, has now the production ability of slaughtering 1.5 to 2 million sheep and 150,000 to 300,000 cattle. Besides, the Delisi and Yuanda groups also strengthen themselves by utilizing their meat resources.

Potato and potato products. Inner Mongolia is a major production base of potatoes. It is also an important base of poison-free potatoes and potatoes for commercial uses. The annual output of potatoes is 6 billion kg. The Ulanqab League in central Inner Mongolia is an ideal place to grow potatoes because of cool climate and big temperature difference between day and night. It is the largest potato production base of the autonomous region, producing one half of the region's total, which accounts for one tenth of the China's total. Each fall, many business people come from other places of China to see and order potatoes. They call the Ulanqab "Kingdom of Potatoes Beyond the Great Wall." Based on potato production, Ulanqab carried out a

Red deer

Kingdom of Green Food

Chinese herbaceous peony

Hedgehog fungus

Saline cistanche

"seed project" and cultivated poison-free potato seedling base and breeding system. Consequently, the fine seed research level of the league leads the world. The potato processing industry also develops rapidly. Nailun Group, after introducing in advanced technological equipment from the world, has set up a refined starch company with an annual production ability of 20,000 tons. Now, it has invested another 100 million yuan to build another plant of the same kind. The potato processing industry has brought abundant profits not only to producers and sellers but also to local farmers.

Other food grains and beans. Naked oats, one of the three "treasures" of Inner Mongolia, mainly grows in Ulanqab, with an annual output of 150 million kg. The naked oats is a highly nutritious food, with rich protein, vitamins and rough fibers, and can prevent arteriosclerosis, coronary heart disease, hypertension and diabetes. It is sold to Beijing, Shanxi and Hebei.

Each summer, all plants grow well in Ulanqab. On hill slopes are white bands of buckwheat. When autumn comes, the white will turn pink. Then farmers will pull them out from the root. Each year, the league can produce 23 million kg of buckwheat. The buckwheat is also highly nutritious: It has chlorophyll and rutin not found in other grains and the content of VB1 and VB2 is four times that of other flours. It can relax belly and reduce high blood pressure and sells well in Japan and the Korean Peninsula.

What's more, the pea, kidney bean and broad bean produced in the region are also of nutritious value and health care function. They are more and more loved by consumers.

Protecting the Green Food

To guarantee the healthy development of green industries, Inner Mongolia Green Food Development Center drew out the Regulations on Production of Green Food Rice, Regulations on Production of Green Food Wheat and Regulations on the Production of Vegetables in Green Food Protection Area. Compared with the international rules on green food, these regulations are more detailed and stricter. Of the 12 leagues and cities of the autonomous region, eight have set up green food management agencies, strengthening the work of production supervisor, quality attestation, technology promotion and personnel training in green food. Also, complete systems of environment supervision, quality attestation and market management have been set up, enhancing the supervision of whole-process green food

78 enterprises engaged in green food production

176 products with green food brand

production, especially the supervision over the standards of production materials, technology, craftsmanship and product quality as well as the package, storage, transportation and freshness keeping of the products. In this way, the standards and quality of green food can be guaranteed and the production can be more standardized, scientific and in a more legal way. The Green Good Development Center issues "green cards" to farmers who want to apply for a production base for green food, on which are printed the number of fertilizer and farm chemical allowed to be used. And regular investigation and guidance will be done. The "green cards" have set up a contract between enterprises and farmers, thus guaranteeing the quality of the raw materials.

It is the basis for the development of green food to control pollution, protect environment and develop ecological agriculture. Each place pays great attention to the protection and construction of ecological environment and links it with the environment protection, including the protection of grassland, forest and farming land. The region properly uses the underground water, realizes water-saving irrigation and improves the utilization rate of water. Also, it pays much attention to the appropriate use of fertilizer, farm chemicals and preventive measures of insect pests, in an aim to reduce the pollution to environment. In setting up new industries, Inner Mongolia attaches great importance to the prevention of the three wastes (waste gas, waste water and industrial residue), thus securing the production of green food.

Bright Future of the Kingdom of Green Food

In implementing the strategy of western development, Inner Mongolia pays much attention to the construction of green food bases and cultivation

Farmers set up ostrich raising field

Raising base of fatty cattle

of leading enterprises and famous brands. In the future, it will continue the efforts in developing the beef and mutton and dairy product bases centering on Hulun Buir, Xilin Gol, Horqin, Ulanqab, Erdos and Urad grasslands, the wheat, rice, corn, bean and fruit and melon production bases in Hetao, Tumochuan, West Liaohe River and West Bank Plain of Nenjiang River, the potato, other grain and bean production bases in the central and west hilly areas, the aquatic products base in Dalai Lake, Dali Nur and Daihai Lake, the mineral water, beverage, edible wild herb production base in the Greater Hinggan Mountains and the vegetable, egg, milk and bird meat

Watermelon going into market

production bases in Hohhot, Baotou, Chifeng and Wuhai. Particular supports will be given to a group of green food processing enterprises so as to enlarge their scales and enhance their scales. By 2010, one third of Inner Mongolia's land will be cultivated into green food plantation area. The green food will account for 40 percent of the agricultural produce and livestock products of the whole region.

In implementing the western development strategy, Inner Mongolia attaches great importance to the development of bio-technology. Using the bio-technology, the autonomous region conducted the embryo transfer and pedigree breeding and introduced and promoted a series of fine breeds in agriculture, livestock, bird and grass. Through the bio-technology, a group of healthy and nutritious food and biological medicines processed from the blood and embryo of animals. At the present stage, the embryo is often thrown away in animal processing. Once handled by high-tech, its value is several or dozes of times more than a sheep or a cattle. The high-tech "Jinshuangqi" abstracted from mutton and beef has special function in medical care. It has been listed as the first-class new medicine and achieved

Ice cream of Ili

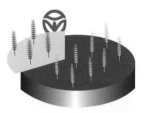

By 2010, the green food plantation area will account for one third of the whole region

Green food accounts for over 40 percent of the agricultural produce of the whole region

good economic and social profits.

Meanwhile, the autonomous region will cultivate its green food processing industries. Through high-tech development, the raw material produced here will double or even multiple its value. Therefore, Inner Mongolia will put great efforts in cultivating green food processing industries, especially the ones crossing provinces and connecting several trades. It will try to establish famous brands in green food production. In this process, the market development is of vital importance. To develop new markets, it has to cultivate a group of famous brands at first. Then, it needs to pay attention of commercial circulation and train a large number of businessmen. At the same time, market sale is important. Both production bases and enterprises have to do research in sales and organize a sales team. Only in this way, can they form a sales network as well as monopoly stores and after-sale service systems in China and even the whole world.

Kingdom of Green Food

6 Rare Earth Industry Opens A New Economic Chapter

Rare Earth Reserves Lead the World

*T*he Bayan Obo Iron Mine is a rare vein containing iron, rare earth and niobium located 150 km north of Baotou. The mine supplies the iron ore for the Baotou Iron and Steel Complex. It is not surprising that Bayan Obo means "richly endowed mountain" in Mongolian.

It is verified that Bayan Obo boasts five veins. It is 16 km long from east to west and two to three km wide from south to north, covering an area of 4,800 hectares. It has verified reserves of more than 1 million tons of iron ore. The reserves of rare earth lead the world, while those of niobium are second only to Brazil. In addition, the mountain contains 142 minerals and

72 chemical elements including quartz, phosphorus, magnesium, potassium, clay and gold.

Rare earth is a functional material of the 21st century, which is closely related with high-tech industries, and Baotou is known in the world as the "rare earth valley. " The rare earth contains 17 chemical elements, of which

(1999, Unit: 10,000 tons)

	World	China	Baotou	Percent of Baotou in the World	Percent of Baotou in China
Industrial reserves	4482	3600	3300	73.6	91.6
Potential reserves	11160	10000	8500	76	85
Output volume	7.5	6.6	4.5	60	68

15 are the lanthanum series starting from the No. 57: lanthanum, cerium, praseodymium, neodymium, promethium, samarium, europium, gadolinium, terbium, dysprosium, holmium, erbium, thulium, ytterbium and lutetium. The other two are yttrium and scandium of the third sub-group. According to the physical and chemical differences between chemical elements, people divide rare earth into two groups: One is called light rare earth or cerium group, including the first seven lanthanum series elements; the other is heavy rare earth or yttrium, including the other eight lanthanum series

Iron, niobium and rare earth mine in Bayan Obo

elements and yttrium and scandium.

Rare earth was discovered in 1794 by a Finnish scientist. In fact, rare earth is not earth at all. It is only a group of typical metal elements, and is less active only to alkali metal and alkaline-earth metal. Further more, rare earth is not rare. The potential rare earth deposit is 100 million tons, which can be used for more than 1,000 years.

Bayan Obo has the largest deposit of rare earth and the second largest deposit of niobium in the world

This is the foundation that rare earth can be used on a large scale in high-tech field. The verified reserves of rare earth in the world are 45 million tons, of which 33 million tons are in Baotou. Please see the table in previous page.

China produces two thirds of the world rare earth. In 1999, it exported 50,000 tons of rare earth and used 16,000 tons. While the total consumption of the rare earth that year was 75,000 tons. China supplies 88 percent of the

Junggar open coal mine

rare earth to the world, which comes mainly from Baotou.

Rare earth was firstly used into metallurgy. If it is added to steel, the strength, resistance to oxidation and wearability of the steel can be strengthened. If it is added to cast iron, the iron can become tougher. If it is added to aluminum wire, the

Mining field of iron and stannum in Huanggang

electric conduction, strength and processing ability of the wire can be enhanced. If it is put into the aluminum, magnesium, zinc, nickel, titanium and bronze, a special kind of alloy can be produced. Also, by utilizing the active character of the rare earth, people also make flint and all kinds of military igniting alloy.

In agriculture, the rare earth can be used as physiological regulator. With some rare earth fertilizer put into farm land, the output of grain and economic plants can be increased. At present, some forage containing rare earth element is used in animal raising, with high profit.

With the transfer of global economic growth pattern and rapid development of high-tech industries, the rare earth has seen wider and wider application in high-tech field. The rare earth new materials having been industrialized include fluorescence, permanent magnetism, polishing compound, hydrogen storage and automobile gas purifier and catalyst.

Now six categories of rare earth products have been formed in Inner Mongolia. They are refined rare earth ore; rare earth, silicon and iron alloy and rare earth, silicon, magnesium and iron alloy; rare earth chloride and carbonic acid rare earth; sole rare earth oxide and metal; mixed rare earth metal and flint; and permanent magnetic materials as neodymium, iron and boron. Over 200 specifications rare earth products in 80 species are sold to

Arxan oil field

more than 20 countries and regions including France, Japan, Germany, the United States and Australia.

Rare earth production enterprises are scattered in Baotou, Hohhot, Wuhai and Bayan Nur League, with major ones in Baotou. For example, the Rare Earth High-Tech Shareholding Co., Ltd, the largest rare earth alloy manufacturer Sanfeng Rare Earth Company and Sino-foreign joint venture Baotou Qingmei Tianjiao Polishing Powder Company are all famous rare earth enterprises under the Baotou Iron and Steel Complex. Also, the largest rare earth institute has also been set up in Baotou.

In carrying out the western development strategy, the rare earth industry will strengthen ties with domestic and foreign enterprises, colleges and scientific research institutes. The aim is to build Inner Mongolia into the largest base of rare earth raw material, rare earth functional material and relevant industries of China and even the whole world.

The Chinese government developed Bayan Obo to develop iron and steel industry. Through 50 years of construction, Inner Mongolia has become a modern iron and steel base. In April 1953, China decided to build a large iron and steel complex in Baotou. The project was one of the key construction projects of the First Five-Year Plan period (1953-1957). The complex produced the first smelted iron on September 26, 1959, putting an end to Inner Mongolia's history of having no iron. On May 1, 1960, the complex turned out its first smelted steel. The establishment and development of the Baotou Iron and Steel Complex played an important role in the improvement of distribution of China's iron and steel industries, the growth of metallurgical production and the development of the local economy. At present, the complex has a total asset volume of 24.6 billion yuan, with an annual production of iron and steel respectively at 4 million tons and over 3 million tons of steel products. Now there are 1,002 specifications of iron and steel products in 38 species, all of high quality. The special alloyed steel produced by North Heavy Industry Group Co., Ltd. has reached the world advanced level. Now the iron and steel industry of Inner Mongolia has formed a comparably complete production system covering mining, ore dressing, sintering, iron smelting, steel smelting, cogging and cold rolling. Also a complete iron and steel industrial system covering geological survey, design, scientific research and construction. It is one of the top ten iron and steel bases of China.

Energy Valley of the New Century

Inner Mongolia boasts an opencut coal-bearing stratum stretching tens of kilometers along the Yellow River in the southeast of the Erdos Plateau. Surprised by its large size, many visitors called it a rare treasure of the world. President of an American commercial group once said to his Chinese partner, "You are sleeping right on top of a gold mine. " This is the Junggar Coal Field. The deep layers are very shallow to the surface. This will allow for ease in strip-mining. Proven deposits total 26.8 billion tons, more than enough to create a coal production base capable of 50 million tons each year. This will also serve as a new base when China begins to shift coal mining from east to west. As some people say, the mine is a window to the Inner Mongolia coal

One out of four lights in Beijing is lit with the electricity transmitted from Inner Mongolia

industry. Over the past decade, China has built five large-scale opencut coal mines. Four of these are located in Inner Mongolia-Junggar, Huolinhe, Yiminhe and Yuanbaoshan-each with deposits of more than 5 billion tons.

Both the proven and prospective coal deposits in the autonomous region rank second in China. To date, a complete coal industrial system has been formed, which combines large-, medium- and small-scale mines and includes geological survey, design, construction, machinery manufacture and scientific research. Major coal bases are found in Ih Ju, Hulun Buir, Chifeng, Wuhai and Huolin Gol, which provide coal to large-scale electric power, iron and steel and chemical enterprises. Coal industry has become a pillar of the economic development of the autonomous region.

Abundant coal resources have laid a solid foundation for the development of power production. The coal mines are mainly concentrated on river belts, especially along the Yellow River, 840 km of which run through the region. The location of the coal mines at the hub of the northeast, northwest and north power grids--three key power facilities of the nation, provides conditions for the development of large-scale power stations near coal mines and transmitting electricity to areas outside the region. The amount of electrical output per capita in Inner Mongolia leads the nation. Its supply meets the demand not only for the region, but also for Beijing and the neighboring country of Mongolia. During the night, Beijing is covered with myriad twinkling lights, one out of four is lit by electricity originating in Inner Mongolia.

Along with China's shifting from east to west in the exploitation of energy resources, Inner Mongolia has made advances in power industry by adopting a strategy of changing supply of coal into transmission of electricity. By the end of 1999, there had been 54 power plants with installed capacity of 6,000 kw or above. The total installed capacity reached 8.64 million kw. They are mainly thermal power plants, while water and wind generated power accounts for only 1.15 of the total. The installed capacity of water power is 205,900 kw. Wanjiazhai hydropower pivot, the first hydropower station on the trunk of the Yellow River, was jointly built by the Ministry of

Water Resources, Shanxi Province and Inner Mongolia Autonomous Region. In 1999, it turned out 610 million kwh of electricity. There are 112 wind power machines, with installed capacity of 46,750 kw. In 1999, the electricity generated through wind power was 91 million kwh. Four wind power stations-Huiteng Xil, Zhurihe, Xilin and Shangdu-have joined the West Inner Mongolia grid, with the second largest installed capacity of its kind in China.

At present, Inner Mongolia has formed east and northeast power grid, north Xilin Gol grid, Lingxi grid of Hulun Buir League, forest grid in Greater Hinggan Mountains and west grid of the autonomous region. The west Inner Mongolia has completed the 800-km long, 220-kv two way net from the Haibowan Power Plant in the west to the Fengzhen Power Plant in the east, which is then connected with north China grid by 550 kv transmission line and 220 kv transmission line respectively in Fengwan and Fengda. While guaranteeing the power supply to the region itself, it also sends electricity to north China. Now the highest power transmission ability is 938,000 kw. In 1999, it transmitted 6.708 billion kwh of electricity to north China. In western development, the power construction in Inner Mongolia will turn its focus from only on electricity source to on the alliance of electricity source construction, grid construction and development of market. The autonomous region will also put forward the union of coal, power, metallurgy and chemicals and set up Wuhai and Baotou industrial gardens, with the aim to build Inner Mongolia into the "energy valley" of China in the 21st

The designed installed capacity of Dalate power plant is the largest in Asia

century.

Heavy-Duty Vehicles Are Booming

Machinery industry based on heavy-duty motor vehicles is an important industry of Inner Mongolia. The manufacturing of heavy-duty motor vehicles emerged and flourished in the 1980s and 1990s. The North-Mercedes Benz Auto Manufacturing Company, by introducing production technology from the German Mercedes Benz Company, can produce 6,000 8-20 tons heavy -duty motor vehicles. It is one of the three heavy-duty motor vehicle manufacturers in China. The North Heavy-Duty Automobile Co., Ltd, founded with investment from Britain and the United States, has developed 13 kinds of auto-unloading mining vehicles in seven types from 23 to 100 tons, which have obtained the quality certificates of ISO9001-1994, ISO9002-1994 and UKS of Britain. It is the only manufacturer in China able to produce auto-unloading mining trucks. In the Three Gorges Project, the trucks have played a big role and got many praises.

Through 50 years of development, the Inner Mongolia machinery industry has developed from small scale to large scale and has formed a

Oil refinery plant
of Hohhot

machinery industrial system centering on heavy-duty motor vehicles (including auto parts) and composed of farming and livestock machines, electric appliances, heavy-duty mining machines, machine

Herdsmen get light and watch TV through solar energy

tools, universal petrochemical equipment, basic machines and other special-purpose machines. The autonomous region has the ability to produce 6,000 automobiles, 2,000 refitted trucks, 30,000 tractors and farming transport vehicles, 6,000-ton boilers, 3,000 metal cutting machine tools, 1,000 forging equipment, 1 million kw electrical machinery, 2 million kv electrical transformer, 5,000-km electrical cable, 10,000 tons of naked lines and other auxiliary parts worth 800 million yuan.

In western development process, Inner Mongolia will stress the development of North-Mercedes Benz and North Heavy-Duty Auto. Meanwhile, it will greatly develop the machine tool parts and electrical engineering and electrical appliances. It will also actively develop large-scale machinery for grass sowing, irrigation, grass raking and bundling and green grass storage, machinery for milking, shearing

Quality supervisors are testing the quality of steel pine produced by Baotou Seamless Steel Pipe Plant

and dairy product processing, special transport vehicles for husbandry, and machinery for livestock product collecting, processing and transporting and wind power machinery. A sales center for agricultural machinery will be set up, thus turning machinery a pillar industry of Inner Mongolia.

Petrochemical Industry Is Rising

Inner Mongolia is abundant in petrochemical resources. It has proven 13 big oil and natural gas fields. The total petroleum is estimated between two to three billion tons, while the deposits of natural gas might be 270-1,000 billion cubic meters. The major body of Shaanxi, Gansu and Ningxia Oil and Gas Field is in the Erdos Basin of Inner Mongolia. The reserves of chemical raw material, natural alkali, sulfur and iron core, phosphorus, limestone, rock with zinc and alumstone are rich. Many lakes in Mu Us and Hobq deserts contain natural alkali, which is called "coral of great deserts". The natural alkali lake groups are all in the Erdos Plateau. Now 19 such lake groups have been discovered, with proven deposits of over 60 million tons and industrial deposits of 6.905 million tons.

To date, a petrochemical industrial system has been formed in Inner Mongolia, which centers on raw material industry and includes petroleum chemical, saline-alkali-niter chemical, fine chemical, coal chemical, chemical machinery and chemical research. The products have developed from the only inorganic chemical material to over 600 species such as the chemical mine, chemical fertilizer, farm chemicals, soda ash, chloric alkali, inorganic salt, organic chemical material, compound material, coating, auxiliary, rubber and chemical machinery. Since 1985, in particular, a large number of large and medium-sized key projects have been finished, including the 500,000-ton natural alkali developing and processing project in Qagan Nur, 1 million crude oil processing project of Hohhot Refinery Plant, 200,000-ton heavy alkali project in Jilantai, 300,000-ton compound ammonia project of the Inner Mongolia Fertilizer Plant, and 520,000-ton urea project.

The Tanyaokou sulfur-iron mine with an annual capacity of sifting 1.2 million tons of ores will be completed soon. These industries have promoted the petrochemical development and enhance the economic strength of the autonomous region, laying a solid foundation for turning petrochemical a pillar industry of the region.

Big petrochemical enterprises can be found in Ih Ju, Baotou and Wuhai. The Ih Ju Chemical Industrial Enterprise Group is the largest chemical industry of China, which majors in the production of inorganic salt and processing of natural alkali. It is a key state-owned enterprise of China and once won the "Global Award" in Chinese fine chemical enterprises. Now it possesses 30 production enterprises, with a total asset of 4.3 billion yuan, 16,000 employees and 1,800 technicians. Of all the products, the sodium bicarbonate and vulcanized alkali possess a relatively large proportion in domestic market. It has set up sales agencies in 20 provinces, municipalities or autonomous regions and enjoys foreign trade autonomy, with its products selling to over 20 countries and regions of Asia, Europe and America. The annual sales volume goes over 1 billion yuan and the foreign currency earned each year is about US$ 20 million.

While continuing the business in natural alkali, the Ih Ju Chemical Industrial Enterprise Group also expands into the field of natural gas. It has

Production line of Shiqi Suit, a famous brand in home and abroad now been confirmed as a launching enterprise of natural gas development by the people's government of Inner Mongolia. It is preparing the pipe transmission of natural gas in western Inner Mongolia and methyl alcohol processing project. On this basis, it plans to set up a chemical natural gas limited company.

Another petrochemical enterprise in the autonomous region is in Baotou, which is now under construction. With a total investment of nearly 10 billion yuan, the enterprise is planned to produce 300,000 tons of synthetic fertilizer, 520,000 tons of urea, 300,000 tons of methyl alcohol and 200,000 tons of acetic acid each year and 500,000 cubic meters of coal gas daily.

Wuhai in west Inner Mongolia is a newly-emerging petrochemical city. The first state-owned enterprise of the region, Wuhai Chemical Plant, was set up in the 1950s. Through a decade's effort between 1985 and 1995, in particular, the chemical industry develops vigorously. Headed by Wuhai Chemical Plant, a chemical industrial system has been formed, which composes of the Yellow River Chemical Plant, Wuda Chemical Industry Company, Wuhai Organic Chemical Plant and Wuhai Electrical Plant. Wuhai

The ratio of high-grade products in Baotou Ludian (Group) Co., Ltd. leads the country

has become a large chemical base of such organic chemical intermediates as coke, caustic soda, soda ash and polyvinyl chloride (PVC) and other chloric products and basic chemical materials as charcoal. As the Wuhai chloric soda project is soon finished, the chemical industry of Wuhai will step onto a new stage in Inner Mongolia's western development.

The newest type of bulldozer TV230 developed by No. 1 Machinery Plant of Inner Mongolia

Nonferrous Metal Industry Has a Bright Future

Since 1985, Inner Mongolia put a large amount of money and efforts in the field of nonferrous metal. It renovated and expanded the Bayin Nur lead and zinc mine, Huogeqi bronze mine, Bainaimiao bronze mine and Tongshun Group and set up the Baotou Bronze Plant and Chifeng Metallurgical Plant. A system combining mining, ore dressing, metallurgy and processing has been perfected. A nonferrous metal framework, represented by lead, zinc and tin in the east and aluminum, magnesium and bronze in the west has basically taken the shape. Technological equipment has seen great improvement.

Inner Mongolia Aluminum Electricity (Group) Co., Ltd is a typical nonferrous metal enterprise. It is one of the eight aluminum plant of China and the only large electrolysis aluminum plant of the autonomous region.

The Baotou Aluminum Plant was founded in 1958 and produced aluminum the next year. The second-stage project was put into operation in 1988. At present, it has an annual production ability of 80,000 tons of aluminum ingot, 58,000 tons of carbon products and 3,000 tons of aluminum moulds. The ratio of first-class quality products is over 95 percent, the highest one of the top 10 aluminum plants in China. The rare earth aluminum produced here was approved as a state-level new product in 1995. The spectrum sample of rare earth aluminum alloy pioneered the country, which was confirmed to be at the state standard by the State Standard Bureau. The product sells well not only in other places of China, but also in the United States and Japan.

In the western development, the nonferrous metal industry follows the principles of high starting point, high standard and high technological content and focuses on the deep processing of aluminum, bronze, lead, zinc, tin and magnesium. By establishing the Baotou Aluminum Electricity Group, Tongshun Group, Chifeng Hongfeng Nonferrous Metal Group and West Bronze Group, Inner Mongolia has fully promoted the enterprise development and created a group of famous brand products representing the production level of nonferrous metal in the region. Over 90 percent of such enterprises are concentrated and the value of famous brands exceed 70 percent. The resource advantages in nonferrous metal will soon become economic advantages.

Coal-to-electricity transmission enables the transportation of coal by air

Table of Mineral Resources in Inner Mongolia Autonomous Region

No.	Name of (Sub-)Minerals	Preserving places	Scale			Reserves		Mining conditions			Note
			Large	Middle	Small	Potential value (100 million yuan)	Rank in China	mining/infrastructure	stopped	closed	
1	coal	332	94	57	181	115165.07	2	218	14	10	I1
2	petroleum	3		1	2	85.74	11				
3	oil shave	5		1	4	8.11	9				
4	iron	81	3	18	60	781.27	7	28	8		I4
5	manganese	7			7	1.01	16	2			A3
6	chromium	7		1	6	9.73	2	5	2		
7	copper	50	1	7	42	180.02	6	18			I12A12
8	lead	40	2	7	31	14.25	3	14	2		I26A6
9	zinc	46	6	15	25	87.8	2	16	2		I20A6
10	bauxite	1			1	0.08	19				I1
11	nickel	2			2	1.7	13				
12	cobalt	5		1	4	0.38	18	1			A5
13	wolfram	15	1	3	11	27.09	10	5	4		A2
14	tin	8	1	4	3	30.82	5	5			I1A4
15	bismuth	4		1	3	7.52	5	1			A4
16	molybdenum	12	1	1	10	58.24	7	2			I5A5
17	antimony	1			1	0.01	16	1			
18	metals of platinum family	8			8	1.17	8				A6
19	gold	152	2	14	136	45.93	10	113	5	10	A18
20	silver	44	3	9	32	42.17	5	22	2		I3A30
21	niobium	6	5		1	2639.77	1	2			I4A1
22	tantalum	1	1			162.75	2				A1
23	beryllium	2	1		1	63.44	2				A1
24	zirconium	1	1			1877.99	1				A1
25	rare earth	8	6		2	809.00	1	2	1	1	I3A2
26	germanium	1			1	0.32	11	1			A1
27	gallium	2			2	6.97	16				A2
28	indium	6		6		11.27	4	2			A6
29	cadmium	13	2	6	5	11.47	7	4	1		A13
30	selenium	2			2	0.04	16	1			A2
31	tellurium	1			1	0.01	15				A1
32	red pillar stone	1			1	0	8	1			
33	common fluorite	26	1	5	20	11.57	3	16	10		
34	gray rock used as flux	5	2	1	2	64.67	10	3			I1
35	dolomite used in metallurgy	5	2	2	1	42.55	13	1			
36	quartz rock used in metallurgy	4		3	1	11.97	8		1		
37	sand stone used in casting molding	3		2	1	0.67	3	2			
38	sand used in casting molding	7	2	5		5.11	2	6			
39	vein quartz used in metallurgy	5		1	4	2.35	3		1		
40	refractory clay	12	1	5	6	108.01	3		2		I1
41	iron alumina	2		1	1	4.25	2				I2
42	sulfur iron	15	4	6	5	381.51	3	3		2	I8
43	associated sulfur iron	6			6	8.85	19	1	1		A6
44	mirabilite	20	3	9	8	8143.75	3	13	1	1	I4
45	natural alkali	9	1	2	6	142.12	2	6	1	1	A1

Table of Mineral Resources in Inner Mongolia Autonomous Region

No	Name of (Sub-)Minerals	Preserving places	Scale			Reserves		Mining conditions			Note
			Large	Middle	Small	Potential value (100 million yuan)	Rank in China	mining/in-frastructure	stopped	closed	
46	gray rock used for producing calcium carbide	2		1	1	6.33	17	1			
47	serpentine rock used for producing fertilizer	2	1		1	23.96	8				
48	gray rock used for producing alkali	2		2		12.44	7				
49	dolomite used in chemical industry	1			1	0.28	4				
50	putty charcoal	5		3	2	0.94	5				
51	salt	9			9	56.48	15	6			I2A1
52	bromine	1			1	0	4				A1
53	arsenic	3	2	1		5.46	4				IIA2
54	boron	1			1	0.03	11				A1
55	phosphorus	10	1	4	5	94.66	11	1		2	I1
56	graphite	13		11	2	8.75	5	7	2		
57	silicon gray stone	1		1		1.40	8				I1
58	mica	15	2	6	7	0.59	3	1	4		
59	garnet rock	4		2	2	0	3	1			
60	vermiculite	1	1			1.98	4		1		
61	zeolite	3	1		2	27.47	2	1			I1
62	gypsum	8	4	2	2	2072.03	2	1			
63	jade stone	1	1			0	7	1			
64	calcite	1			1	0	4				
65	iceland spar	1		1		0				1	
66	gray rock used for producing cement	39	1	13	25	181.47	24	24			I3
67	gray rock used for producing lime	2			2	0.25	3	2			I2
68	quartz rock used for producing glass	1		1		2.13	11				
69	sand rock used for producing glass	1			1	0.66	18				
70	sand used for producing glass	7	3	4		37.76	5	7			
71	sand rock used for producing cement	2		2	1	0.61	20	1			
72	sand used in building	1		1		0.78	5				
73	vein quartz used for producing glass	1			1	2.35	10		1		
74	diatomaceous earth	2		1	1	0	7	1			
75	kaoling earth	7		4	3	5.65	12	3			
76	shale used for producing cement	2			2	0.32	19	1			
77	pottery and porcelain clay	5	1	4		9.46	9	2			
78	pengrun clay	6	1	2	3	54.94	3	2			I1
79	clay used for producing bricks and tiles	4	1	3		25.31	2	2			
80	clay used for producing cement	13	3	4	6	25.48	5	4			I1
81	peridotite used in building	1			1	4.76	1	1			
82	augite rock used in decoration	1			1	0	1	1			
83	diabase used in decoration	1			1	4.38	4	1			
84	granite used in building	1		1		46.47	3				
85	granite used in decoration	3			3	114.23	10	1			
86	marble used in decoration	5		2	3	35.26	23	2			
87	marble used for producing cement	10		2	8	42.32	3	7			I1
88	slate used for producing cement	2	1		1	18.11	1	1			
89	pearlite	2		1	1	3.23	6	1			

Note: The I in the Notes refer to "intergrowing minerals" while A refers to "associated minerals".

International Cooperation and Domestic Alliance

7

*W*ith the implementation of the western development strategy and acceleration of economic globalization, Inner Mongolia has been adjusting its economic structure and altering its foreign trade system and operational ways unfit for the market economy. It is trying to meet the demands of general norms governing international market and has done a lot in import and export, investment attraction, international cooperation, lateral alliance, port construction, development zone construction and inviting businesses and investment, creating a favorable economic and policy environment for investors.

Foreign Trade and Economy with Bright Prospect

Now in Inner Mongolia, 700 enterprises have the right to conduct

Opening ceremony of the meat product fair held in Xilin Hot, Inner Mongolia

business with foreign countries. The business covers cash trade, small-sum trade in frontiers, mutual trade of frontier people, contract project and labor cooperation, utilization of foreign capital, transportation in foreign trade, package and decoration, advertisement and exhibition, etc. A "great trade and economic framework" combining management and operation, import and export and featuring multi-layer, multi-channel and multi-forms of operation has been formed. It has

Building of Bank of China, Inner Mongolia Branch

set up offices in Beijing, Tianjin, Qinhuangdao, Dalian, Guangzhou, Shenzhen, Haikou and Xiamen and trading companies in the United States, Hong Kong, Japan, Russia, Mongolia and eastern European countries. At present, Inner Mongolia has developed trade exchanges and economic and technological cooperation with more than 80 countries and regions, with 300 species of commodities for export. Also, it has developed a group of famous brands and key products, including cashmere, cashmere products, rare earth, carpet, forage, mahuang (Chinese ephedra) element, corn, live

cattle and sheep, buckwheat, fluorine stone, steel products and coal. Of them, over 60 have an annual export volume of over US$1 million and 16, an annual export volume of over US$10 billion. In 1999, the total import and export volume reached US$ 1.61 billion. Meanwhile, the commodity structure of import and export is optimizing year by year. The finished industrial products have seen a higher and higher proportion in export, while that of raw products is decreasing. The imported products have also expanded from traditional machinery equipment, raw material, scientific instrument, medical instrument, spare parts and living necessities to industrial production line and technological innovation equipment. As a result, the production equipment of the whole region is effectively renovated and parts of commodities have been upgraded.

Inner Mongolia is steady in utilizing foreign funds. From 1979 to 1999, the whole region, on an accumulative basis, contracted utilizing foreign funds of US$2.3 billion, involving over 40 countries and regions including the Netherlands, Denmark, Japan, Spain, Canada, the United States, Germany, France, Belgium, Italy, Australia and Hong Kong. The foreign funds are invested in fields of light industry, textile, energy, transportation, chemical industry, building material, metallurgy, medicine, agriculture, husbandry and forestry, machinery, electronics and tertiary industry. This has filled much vigor to the economy, greatly promoted the economic development and opening-up process, relaxed the capital shortage in

International Cooperation and Domestic Alliance

Jinchuan Development Zone of Hohhot

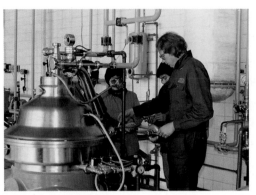

construction and improved the management and technological level in enterprises of the whole region.

Starting from practical conditions of the region and taking advantages of its geographical position, abundant labor resources

US experts are testing the quality of the Sun brand oil

and complementary economy with other countries, Inner Mongolia has greatly launched the contract projects and labor cooperation with others, with the levels improving constantly. The cooperative scope and market are also expanding, involving in plantation, processing, food and restaurant, building decoration, electric power installation, design and consultation. A multi-directional, trans-industrial, multi-layer and high-tech framework has been basically formed.

In recent years, Inner Mongolia has put great efforts in "going abroad. " It actively develops international market, especially the African ones, sets up enterprises and conducts processing trade in foreign countries, thus promoting the adjustment of industrial structure in the region. To date, Inner Mongolia has established more than 200 enterprises in foreign countries including Russia, Mongolia, Madagascar, Germany, France, the United States and South Africa, with a total investment volume of US$40 million. Such enterprises as King Deer and Nationalities Group have achieved good economic profits in other countries and solved the employment problem of the local place.

The carrying out of western development strategy and China's soon entry into World Trade Organization (WTO) provided an unprecedented opportunity for the development of Inner Mongolia's foreign trade and economy. The autonomous region, as a front of China's opening-up in the north, will go on with its opening-up strategy and "Great Trade and Economic Strategy, " accelerate the structure adjustment of export and try to form a new framework of foreign trade, foreign capital utilization and international economic and technological cooperation with Inner Mongolian characteristics. The focus will be on the pillar and pioneering industries of the region and export of corn, cashmere, livestock, meat, rare earth and coal shall be expanded. It plans to reduce the cost of planting corn by introducing high-quality and high-yield seeds as well as advanced production technology from foreign countries and change the export subsidy into subsidies before and during the corn growth. The work to strive for the self export right continues. It will increase the export ration of cashmere and cashmere products in the products of the same kind of all the country from the present 15.46 percent to one third. It will also expand the export of livestock. On the basis of Tongliao, Ulanqab, Xilin Gol and Chifeng, which provide live cattle to Hong Kong, the market will be extended to the Republic of Korea, Japan and Europe. By fully utilizing the non-pollutant grassland, the region strengthens cooperation with both domestic and international businessmen and continuously expands the export of meat product. The production of rare earth deep processing products has also been accelerated, to increase the ration to 30,000 tons. To use its abundant coal resources, Inner Mongolia is striving for the self export right of coal from the state, and a coal export system of its own is being designed.

In the great strategy of western development, Inner Mongolia will further expand its scale of utilizing foreign funds and comprehensively improve the level of its opening-up.

International Cooperation Is Improving

Since the reform and opening-up, Inner Mongolia has established friendly exchanges and trade and economic cooperation with nearly 100 countries and regions. Officials at the ministerial or higher levels from over 20 countries have visited the region. In the wake of the vigorous development of border trade, frontier tourism and contacts between people living along the border have also been promoted. The Republic of Mongolia opened a consulate-general in Hohhot. Twenty-two banners, counties and cities have been designated as open areas. In addition, local cities have established sister-city relations with nine foreign cities: Hohhot with Okazaki of Japan, Hailar with Chita of Russia, Baotou with Orchon of Mongolia and Baotou with El Paso, Texas in the United States.

Inner Mongolia actively promotes international economic and technological cooperation, especially in contract project, labor cooperation, overseas investment and aiding foreign countries project. Good economic and social effects have been achieved, which is beneficial to the opening-up of the region. By the end of 1999, the whole region had signed 1,306 contracts on labor cooperation and design and consultation, involving a total contracted volume of US$756 million. The operation volume completed was

A new busy day begins in Manzhouli Port

US$373 million and 47,791 laborers had been sent out. The business scope has expanded from the initial plantation, forest cutting and medium- and small-size earth construction to the present large and medium-sized construction projects, cable TV, electric power equipment, metallurgical and

Commodity trading fair in Erenhot

chemical design, wool processing, communication, mining, sewing, food and beverage and agricultural and husbandry techniques. The cooperative market has also expanded from Russia and Mongolia to Japan, Romania, Pakistan, Bangladesh, United Arab Emirates and Tanzania. In external help, Inner Mongolia has carried out 10 such items by the end of 1999, involving a total sum of US$9.55 million. The countries receiving aids include Mongolia, Tanzania and Indonesia. The assisting materials include flour, sugar, starch processing, coal mine equipment, plumb and boiler, fire extinguisher, hospital maintenance and building materials.

By employing the multilateral and bilateral assistance, Inner Mongolia has obviously improve the economic status and social appearance of poverty-stricken areas. For example, the Ongniud Banner of Chifeng, on receiving the aid from United Nations Development Program (UNDP), has developed into a model herding field. The Women and Children Health Care Hospital, with the aid of UN World Health Organization (WHO), has improved its medical technology. The Tumd Left Banner of Hohhot has developed agriculture and husbandry with the assistance from the Food and Agriculture Organization (FAO) of the UN. The Hinggan League received the aid from

International Cooperation and Domestic Alliance

109

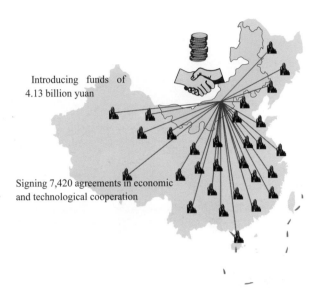

Introducing funds of 4.13 billion yuan

Signing 7,420 agreements in economic and technological cooperation

Building of the People's Insurance Company of China, Inner Mongolia Branch

Australian Government and started protection of grassland. The medical network and equipment in agricultural and pastoral areas are perfected by using the aid from Japanese Government. The No. 2 Middle School of Hohhot, aided by the Japanese Government, has improved its teaching facilities and the nine-year compulsory education. In fighting against floods and rebuilding houses, it also received assistance from the United Nations Children's Fund (UNICEF) as well as those from Australia and Germany. By the end of 1999, Inner Mongolia has benefited from 33 assisting programs of such international organizations as the UNDP, WHO, FAO, United Nations Population Fund (UNFPA) and UNICEF as well as countries as Japan, Germany and Australia and embassies stationed in China. The total money involved is US$41.31 million.

Widening Lateral Economic Ties

By giving full play to its geological advantage of spanning across northeast, north and northwest China and bordering on eight provinces and autonomous regions, Inner Mongolia has formed regional economic cooperative groups with the provinces of northeast China, provinces and municipalities rimming the Bohai Sea, and provinces and autonomous regions along the Yellow River. It has also set up mutual aid relationship with Beijing and Hebei Province, and directed cooperation with a

Carpet production line of Hong Kong Weixin Group Company

large number of coastal cities and provinces, including Tianjin. The autonomous region has so far established economic cooperative ties with 29 municipalities, provinces and autonomous regions as well as a great number of other cities, introduced domestic investment of 4.13 billion yuan, and signed 7,420 economic and technological cooperative projects. Between 1994 and 1995, the region absorbed 600 million yuan from Beijing, Tianjin and Hebei Province, and signed a total of 571 economic and technological cooperative projects with them. In 1994 investment negotiations jointly sponsored by the municipalities and provinces rimming the Bohai Sea, the region signed 61 economic and technological cooperative projects involving

International Cooperation and Domestic Alliance

contracted domestic investment of 128 million yuan. In 1995, the autonomous region organized 45 small economic and trade fairs, in which 256 economic and technological cooperative projects with contracted investment of 1.64 billion yuan were signed. In the past 10-odd years, Inner Mongolia has totally signed 7,630 economic and technological cooperative projects, introducing domestic investments of 5.82 billion yuan.

In carrying out the western development strategy, Inner Mongolia will bring its geographical advantage to the full and further strengthens lateral cooperation with brother provinces, autonomous regions and municipalities. It will enhance cooperation with northeast economic zones, economic zones rimming the Bohai Sea, northwest economic zones and Jiangsu, Zhejiang, Shanghai and Fujian provinces, especially the mutual aid relationship with Beijing. It will destroy the traditional system of local place, pay attention to the rational distribution of resources, actively conduct inter-provincial infrastructure construction such as transportation and communication and key industrial projects, jointly develop tourism resources and jointly form a great market. By joint development, the provinces, autonomous regions and municipalities will form industries on their own advantages, thus perfecting the regional labor division and cooperation. According to the market need and local advantages, each province can decide its own pillar industries and advantageous industries and the head of them and actively develop internal and external combination and merger. Meanwhile, enterprises not in the advantageous industries are encouraged to join enterprise groups of other provinces.

Inner Mongolia has a border line of 4,200 kilometers, along which 18 open ports are scattered. Of them, 11 are at the first-class, while the other seven are of the second-class ones. An open port system boasting rail, highway, sea and air transportation facilities has initially taken shape. Annual handling capacities now exceed 20 million tons.

The general goal of Inner Mongolia in port construction is to realize access to water, electricity, road and telecommunications within three to five years starting from 1999. The key ports such as Manzhouli and Erenhot will be built into the advanced ones of the same kind in China. In line with the policy of the Ministry of Foreign Trade and Economic Cooperation that "giving support to western development, enjoying preferential policies in setting up free economic cooperative zone in border areas than those in coastal areas and relaxing the limits on foreign trade", Inner Mongolia has decided to establish two border free economic cooperative zones in Manzhouli and Erenhot. The direction in the future is to greatly develop port industries, set up export basis in Manzhouli and Erenhot and export commodity wholesale market oriented to Russia and the Republic of Mongolia and imported commodity bonded area as well as vegetable and fruit production and wholesale center also oriented towards the two countries.

Infrastructure construction in port areas should be strengthened. The multiple track of Harbin-Manzhouli Railway will be opened completely, thus fundamentally solving the bottleneck problem in Manzhouli. List the

Exterior of Hetao Hengfeng
Flour Plant

International Cooperation and Domestic Alliance

Night Scene of Hohhot

Zhongqiao Airport project in Manzhouli in the overall planning of western development of the region and open cargo flights to Russia. Build Manzhouli-Hailar high-grade roads. Build the high-grade road linking Erenhot and Tianjin Port and opening the passageway to the sea. Accelerate the road construction between such border ports as Qeh, Ganqimaodao, Zhuen Gadabuqi, Arxan, Ebu Dag and Arihashate and banners and cities. Quicken the step to turn Baotou Railway container transfer station into an inland open port at the state level and brings its role to radiating to Shaanxi, Gansu and Ningxia into full play.

Manzhouli port is in the center of economic circle of northeast Asia. It sits against three northeast provinces of China and east Mongolia and faces Serbia Great Railway of Russia. To its east are fine natural ports as Haishenwai and Nahuode. It is one of the most important and convenient passageway between Asia and Europe. Meanwhile, it is the largest land port in China. The commodity handled here each year is equal to the sum of all other border ports in the country. The railway port, after the expansion in 1990, can handle up to 10 million tons of cargo each year, the most one among all border ports. In 1998, 14 road passages were completed, which can handle 3 million tons of cargo and 3.5 million passengers each year, the second largest one following only the Huanggang Port of Shenzhen. The

Spinning workshop of Hohhot No. 2 Woolen Mill, which has introduced in advanced equipment from abroad

Xinqiao Airport, with approval from the State Council and Central Military Committee, has seen its early-stage project finished, including the water and electricity supply and road leveling. The overall construction will start soon. With regard to oil pipeline, a

116

The tomato jam and tomato pieces produced by Xingye Food Co., Ltd have all been sold to North American and Southeast Asian countries

10-km-long oil pipeline has been completed in the Chinese side and the one in Russian side will start soon. It is designed to transmit 2 million tons of oil each year.

To meet the demand of opening-up, Inner Mongolia has submitted an application to the state to allow Manzhouli to become a frontier free economic cooperative zone. In that case, it can develop bilateral or multilateral economic cooperation with others according to the rules and measures for free trade zone and border economic cooperative area. The major functions of Manzhouli as a frontier free economic cooperative area include: International trade, transit and transit trade, internal trade and trade and consultation service, processing trade (including simple commercial processing), storehouse and transit bonded area, finance and tourism.

Erenhot port is in the due north of China, which looks far into the Zhamenwude of Mongolia. As the only rail port between China and Mongolia, it can annually handle cargo of 3.5 million tons. Also, it is an

important pivot of Eurasia Continental Bridge. Erenhot is widely connected with domestic economic zones. The Jining-Erenhot Railway, centered on Jining, is linked in the east with economic zones rimming the Bohai Sea through Beijing and Tianjin. In the west, it is connected with middle and west development zone through Hohhot and Baotou. In the south, after Datong, it extends to the energy base of Shanxi Province and in the north it joins the Jining-Tonghua Railway

First-class cable produced by Hohhot Cable Plant first and then corresponds with the

economic zones in northeast. The special geographical advantage has provided a wide space for Erenhot to conduct foreign trade and economic activities.

Erenhot will also develop into a frontier free economic cooperative area. Its main functions are: First, stress the development of export-oriented product processing and processing added value industries of imported goods; Second, attract domestic and foreign businessmen to open multi-level and various forms of international trade; Third, open bonded storehouses and commodity display business; Fourth, expand the business scope of finance, insurance and transportation in line with WTO rules and the overall planning of the western development and emphasizes the solution of account settling problems restricting Sino-Mongolian trade development; Fifth, selectively develop some high-tech industries suitable to both the Chinese and

118

Mongolian markets such as bioengineering and green food; and the sixth, form a Sino-Mongolian Trade and Economic Information Center.

Vigorous Development Zones

Inner Mongolia currently has five state-level development zones, namely the Baotou Rare Earth New and High-tech Industries Development Zone, Erenhot Frontier Economic Cooperative Zone, Manzhouli Frontier Economic Cooperative Zone, Manzhouli Sino-Russian Trade Zone and Hohhot Technological Development Zone. The 13 autonomous region-level development zones include Hailar Economic Development Zone, Linhe Economic Development Zone, Hinggan League Arxan Economic and Technological Development Zone, Chifeng Pingzhuang Economic and Technological Development Zone, Chifeng Qiaoxi Development Zone and Chifeng Hongshan Comprehensive Experimental Development Zone. All have finished infrastructure construction, providing electricity, water and gas supply, a water drainage system, a heating system, post and telecommunications facilities, roads and land leveling.

In addition to their advantages of resources, geographical location and advanced techniques, the development zones give preference to domestic and foreign investors, especially in taxation and distribution of profits, development of new and high-tech industries and the exploitation of lands, encouraging them to invest in the local economy. Investment had been attracted mainly from the United States, Japan, the Republic of Korea, Canada, Singapore as well as Hong Kong and Taiwan. The development zones took in investment totaling 1.4 billion yuan, and generated industrial output value of 1.837 billion yuan, profits and taxes of 130 million yuan, and foreign exchange earnings of US$24.698 million. On the basis of state industrial policies that favor the central and western parts of the country, development zones in Inner Mongolia are striving for special and preferential treatment.

International Cooperation and Domestic Alliance

8 Vitalizing Inner Mongolia Through Science and Technology

16,854 teaching staff

49,372 students in universities and colleges

18 institutions of higher learning

*I*nner Mongolia attaches great importance to the role of education, science and technology and talents in economic development and social progress. Therefore, it set the science and technology as the core of vitalizing the autonomous region and put forward that "education is the basis, science and technology must lead the way and talents are the key" in western development strategy. Relying on the achievements in education, science and technology and talents training in the past decades, Inner Mongolia puts more efforts in the basic, higher and vocational education and tries to strengthen the introduction, development, promotion and application of scientific and technological achievements. It is a fundamental policy followed by the autonomous region to keep the present talents, introduce urgently needed talents and train prospective talents.

After 50 years of construction and development, Inner Mongolia has formed a complete educational system covering from preschool education to higher education and vocational and adult education as well as ordinary education.

2,750 persons with senior or above professional certificates

7,671 full-time teachers

16,854 teaching staff in universities and colleges

Higher education with complete subject categories. At present, Inner Mongolia possesses 18 general universities and colleges, with 16,845 teaching and administrative staff members, of whom 7,671 are professional teachers. The number of students in these universities and colleges is 49,732, who major in liberal arts, science, engineering, agriculture, forestry, medicine, teaching, finance, politics, arts and foreign languages. There are two units which can endow doctor's degree in 10 specialties and eight units which can endow master's degree in 101 specialties. The postgraduates number 1,262. In the region, there is a key subject at the state level, two construction subjects for "Project 211" and 35 key subjects at the regional level. The Inner Mongolia University has been listed among the "Project 211." Now the universities and colleges here have set up inter-school links with more than 50 institutes of higher learning and scientific research in the United States, Canada, Australia, Japan, Mongolia and Russia. Joining hands with foreign agencies, Inner Mongolia Normal University has set up the International Modern Designing Art College under it and Inner Mongolia Polytechnic University, a school of business.

The universities and colleges fully utilize their advantages in talents, knowledge and science and technology and actively participate in the economic construction of the state and the autonomous region. To date, they have achieved a lot in many fields. The region boasts 49 research institutes and has 11,300 full-time or part-time research technicians, strong enough to undertake key scientific tasks in different fields and at different levels. In

Vitalizing Inner Mongolia Through Science and Technology

121

both natural sciences and social sciences, some items have got awards from the state, ministries or the autonomous region. Some of the scientific and technological achievements have reached the international or domestic advanced level. In recent years, these universities and colleges have undertaken 800 research programs of the state, autonomous region or enterprises, of which over 200 are new ones of the year. These have created good economic and social profits.

Vocational education in various forms. Through years of efforts, the secondary technical education has expanded and the basic construction of vocational education strengthened. The secondary education level is improving in a steady way. Inner Mongolia has now 105 general secondary professional schools, 84 secondary technical schools and 443 vocational middle schools, with 101,396, 84,579 and 225,891 students respectively. The quality of vocational school teachers improves greatly, and the construction of laboratories and experimental fields also see good

Technicians promoting new technology in the field

achievements. Now there have been 324 bases for training purposes in urban area for vocational school students, 76 in rural areas and 32 in herding areas. Of all of them, four general secondary technical schools and eight vocational middle schools are key ones at the state level, and another 18 and 24 are at the regional or ministerial level. Between 1949 and 1998, these schools have sent out 518,000 graduates.

Basic education stressing overall development. In 1990, Inner Mongolia issued the compulsory education programs of its own and began implementing the nine-year compulsory education. By 1999, 64 banners and counties of the region have realized the goal, covering 58.31 percent of the population. The structure of middle and primary schools becomes more rational, nearly covering all area of the region. There are 10,849 primary schools, enrolling 2.2484 million students; and the figures of general middle schools are respectively 1,710 and 1.18 million. The enrollment rate of school-age students, enrollment rate of school-age girl students and proportion of primary school graduates going to middle school are respectively 99.44 percent, 99.56 percent and 94.5 percent, which surpasses or goes near to the national average level. The numbers of kindergartens and children in them are respectively 1,771 and 340,000. Besides, there are 27 schools for special education, enrolling 3,236 students.

In the western development process, Inner Mongolia will carry out the following five projects: The compulsory education in poverty-stricken areas, expanding enrollment of universities and colleges, cross-century quality education, construction of basic cultural facilities and everybody enjoying basic health care services. In this way, it aims at promoting the educational and cultural quality and health level of the whole nation.

Science and Technology Develops Vigorously

Since its founding more than 50 years ago, especially after the reform and opening-up in the end of the 1970s, Inner Mongolia has rapidly

Vitalizing Inner Mongolia Through Science and Technology

developed its science and technology cause, which plays an important role in the economic development and social progress.

Scientific research system completed. To date, Inner Mongolia has set up 133 research institutes of natural sciences, 99 research agencies jointly created by universities and colleges and large and medium-sized enterprises and over 800 privately-run scientific and technological enterprises. The scientific progress has contributed 33 percent of the total industrial and agricultural output value. Statistics at the end of 1999 show that the autonomous region possessed 822 technology trading units under different ownership, which, on an accumulative basis, have signed 22,890 technological contracts with others, with a total business volume of 2.5 billion yuan. Since the publication of the Patent Law, 7,604 products have applied for patent, and 3,955 been authorized. The implementation of patented technology has brought about 6.7 billion yuan of output value, 1.18 billion yuan of profits and taxation and created US$ 140 million of foreign currency. Of the 46 economic cases involving patent, 45 have been concluded. By the end of 1999, there had been 6,005 scientific and

Inner Mongolia Museum with local characteristics

technological achievements registered, of which 55 have gotten awards from the state and 2,656 from the autonomous region. In the past 20 years, Inner Mongolia has actively conducted scientific and technological exchanges and cooperation with other countries through governmental or non-governmental channels. It has signed cooperative or exchanging agreements with 14 countries and regions, of which 21 are between governments. Also, it has signed more than 40 bilateral or multilateral scientific cooperative agreements or letters of intention. Of the 1,800 students, trainees

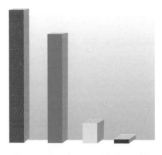

- 10,849 primary schools, with 2.2484 million students
- 1710 general middle schools, with 1.18 million students
- 1,771 kindergartens, with 340,000 children
- 27 schools for special education, with 3,236 students.

and scholars it sent out to overseas, 72 percent have returned upon graduation.

Scientific and technological achievements rich. Great achievements advanced in the world have been made in the field of basic science. In agriculture, Inner Mongolia has cultivated seven wheat breeds suitable for dry land or water-irrigated land, four corn breeds which can replace the former ones and 12 licorice species. All these new breeds have high output and high quality, thus turning 90 percent of major grains in the region fine ones. In husbandry, breakthroughs have been made in new species breeding, cultivating and construction of core groups of fine-wool sheep, meat sheep, white cashmere goat and meat cattle. The breeding of Horqin cattle, selection of fine breeds of white cashmere goat and double-humped camel, development of new kinds of meat sheep and cattle, promotion of highly-efficient family farm model and popularization of model raising technology have turned 66.6 percent of the livestock in the region fine ones. The online supervision research of the wall thickness of the blast furnace leads the country, which has been applied in many large iron and steel enterprises including the Baotou Iron and Steel Complex, Taiyuan Iron and Steel Complex and Capital Iron and Steel Complex. Breakthroughs were also made in the research and promotion of prevention of sunflower, bean and licorice diseases and cattle grub.

High and new technology progressing. The Inner Mongolia Autonomous Region has been paying much attention to the development of high and new technologies and their industrialization. Since the Torch Program was carried out 10 years ago, the region has achieved a lot in high and new technological development. By the end of 1999, the autonomous region has organized 122 items of the "Torch Program", focusing on new materials, biotechnology, electronics and information, machinery and electricity integrity and energy and environment protection. Of these

Satellite launching base in Inner Mongolia

programs, 34 are at the state level and 88 at the regional level. The technologies of test tube sheep, test tube cattle and embryo transplanting of sheep and cattle are advanced either in the world or in China.

The Baotou Rare Earth High-Tech Development Zone is named after the industry it is engaged in. Now the development zone has cultivated a series of programs with high-tech content and economic profits, for example, the rare earth niobium

Multi-media language classroom of the Wuhai No. 1 Middle School

and hydrogen battery, rare earth permanent magnetic engine for motors, rare earth permanent magnetic materials, Mercedes heavy-duty motor vehicles, combing cashmere, electronics and information and fine chemicals. A high-tech industrial group represented by rare earth, electronics and information and machinery and electricity integrity has been basically formed. By the end of 1999, the autonomous region has confirmed 89 high-tech enterprises, of which 59 are in the Baotou Rare Earth High-Tech Development Zone. The Huameng Jinhe (Group) Industrial Co., Ltd, North Heavy-Duty Automobile Co., Ltd. and Rare Earth High-Tech Co., Ltd. under the Baotou Iron and Steel Complex are key high-tech enterprises at the state level.

In carrying out the western development strategy, Inner Mongolia will try to make breakthroughs in system reform, enhance its ability in technological innovation, improve the quality of labors in talents training and increase the contribution of science and technology to economy. In particular, the autonomous region should take full advantages of its plant and animal resources and accelerate the development of bio-chemical

Vitalizing Inner Mongolia Through Science and Technology

127

medicines, new medicine with special-purposes and health care medicines. Also, by employing microorganism and enzyme technology, it will develop high-grade food addictive and new forage addictive. By embryo transplant and artificial insemination, it will speed up the improvement of animals. Besides, it will promote the implementation of biotechnology project.

Talent Team and Talents Training

Inner Mongolia attaches great importance to the use and development of talented people and looks on human resources as the most important of all. It is one of the important measures of the autonomous region to bring the talents into full play and introduce talents from other places, thereby providing human resources guaranty for the western development.

Talent team has a strong lineup. Since 1978 when China began reform and opening-up, the professional and technical team of Inner Mongolia has been expanding, with its number increasing, quality improving, structure more rational and age and cultural structure perfecting. It can basically meet the construction demand of the autonomous region. By the end of 1999, the autonomous region had possessed 504,000 professionals

Inner Mongolia Library

The autonomous region possesses 504,000 professionals and technicians

25,000 have got the senior professional certificate

152,900 have got professional titles of middle rank.

and technicians, accounting for 21.3 percent of the region's total population. Of them, 25,000, or 5 percent, have got the senior professional certificate, and 152,900, or 30.3 percent, have got professional titles of middle rank.

Among the talented people at the higher level, there is one academician, 23 supervisors of Ph. D. candidates, 1,234 persons with senior professional certificates, 1,700 persons with a master's degree or above, 1,400 returned students, 48 youths appraised as experts with outstanding contributions at the state-level, 259 youths appraised as experts with outstanding contributions at the regional level, 1,008 experts enjoying special pensions of the government, 477 technicians making great contributions and 11 persons have been elected to the talent project of the country. In the talent project of the autonomous region, 36 persons have been selected to be the first-class talents and 236, the second-class ones. The team of management talents is also strengthening, now with 84,914 members.

Create favorable conditions to attract talented people. Inner Mongolia put many efforts in training academic leaders with internationally advanced level and key young members in scientific research to tackle thorny problems and in the construction of key subject and key laboratories. It is expanding the channels to attract talents

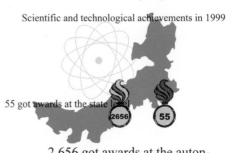

Scientific and technological achievements in 1999

55 got awards at the state level

2,656 got awards at the autonomous region level

from both home and abroad. Talents to be introduced are academicians with Chinese Academy of Sciences (CAS) and Chinese Academy of Engineering (CAE), persons with a master's or doctor's degree, professionals and technicians urgently needed in economic development; leaders of high-tech industries, key projects and new subjects; professionals and technicians with personal invention, patent and technological achievements; and high-level management talents. Inner Mongolia guarantees the legal income of scientific and technological researchers in profit distribution. Government agencies can transfer the scientific and technological results of professional technicians, who can draw no less than 20 percent of the net income after the technological transformation as an award. Those producing economic profits by using their own technology, project and patent can get award from the government as well as the reward of the institution they work for according to contract. The government will give special award to those having obtained the first- or second-class award of national natural sciences

Family reading room of herdsmen

and state fine teaching award. The government allots a subsidy of 3,000 yuan per month to academicians of the CAS and CAE, 1,000 yuan to tutors of Ph. D. candidates, 400 yuan to professionals and technicians with the titles of senior rank and 300 yuan to Ph. D. candidates. Government of all levels

Fine breed milk cow settle down in Inner Mongolia

and units will also provide to high-level talents and returned students with starting fund of scientific projects and essential working conditions. The talented people introduced will enjoy health care services, housing and transportation. Postgraduates and returned students, if work in Inner Mongolia, can be accompanied by their spouses and children.

To develop knowledge economy and realize scientific and technological innovation, Inner Mongolia accelerates its steps in the training, development, use and management of talents. By setting up and innovating scientific mechanism of using people, it can sort out excellent persons. By setting up and innovating talent circulation mechanism, it can best realize the combination of talents and economic construction. By setting up and innovating mechanism for talent training and introduction, it can continuously improve the innovation level of these people. By setting up and innovating talent encouraging mechanism, it can arouse people's enthusiasm and creativity to the greatest degree. By setting up and innovating talent evaluation mechanism, it can create favorable conditions for the talents in market competition. Only when effective measures are taken in keeping the present talents, introducing new talents and training talents for the future, can a large talent team be established.

Great Scene of Inner Mongolia

*T*he scenes in the east and west Inner Mongolia are totally different. In its east is the vast sea of Greater Hinggan forest and its west, the great desert. Besides, there are numerous rivers, lakes, volcanoes and warm springs favorable for tourism development. The tourism structure of the region is based on great grasslands and supplemented by mountains, water, forest and desert.

The broad grassland is the most special one in the scene of Inner

Mongolia. The major body of the grassland spans across a large area, from the Hulun Buir in the northeast to the Alxa desert in the west. The vegetation keeps well. The Erdos Plateau in the southern tip of Inner Mongolia grassland is mostly desert because of the topography, climate and soil there. From the east to the west, the grassland of the region can be categorized into four groups: The typical grassland, grassy marshland, arid grassland and desert grassland. Major grasslands include the Hulun Buir, Horqin, Xilin Gol and Ulanqab grasslands. The Hulun Buir and Xilin Gol grasslands are the best and the most famous ones. A kind of plant, with blossom first and then leaves, will greet the spring in snow each year. In summer, the green grass, flowers and cattle and sheep flocks will compose a beautiful picture.

The Greater Hinggan Mountains has a total forest area of 6.67 million hectares. The ecological environment is preserved well. The beautiful mountains and rivers and diversified species of wild animals provide favorable conditions for the development of sightseeing industry here.

In the west part of Inner Mongolia, the area of Gobi desert reaches 200,000 square km. The deserts there such as Badain Jaran, Tengger, Ulan Buh, Mu Us and Hobq are full of mysteries. The sandy hills, oases and

Great gathering at Nadam Fair

Monastery of Genghis Khan

lakes make up a unique natural scene. The Xiangshawan (Singing Sand Bay) in the Hobq Desert on the southern bank of the Yellow River is one of the three sand-singing areas of China. The Daqinggou (Great Green Ditch), winding its way across the Horqin Desert, houses many kinds of broadleaf trees rarely found in north China. It is an ideal place for professional investigation and tourism. What's more, there are four great scenes in the deep forest of Oroqen, the legendary Gaxian Cave, Tianchi (Pool of the Heaven) and Dujuan (Azalea) Lake.

Of the thousands of rivers in Inner Mongolia, the Yellow River is the longest, which covers 800 km of Inner Mongolia and brings many conveniences to the region, such as irrigation, navigation, electricity generation and fishing. As the Yellow River flows from south to north into Inner Mongolia, it forms a special phenomena-"ice run". It happens each winter when the river gets frozen and each spring when the river melts. Ergun River is another big river in Inner Mongolia, which is 540 km long. It is called Hailar River in the upper reach and receives the branches of Miandu, Mori Gol and Yimin rivers to become a border river between China and Russia. Other famous rivers include the Nenjiang River and West Liaohe River.

Inner Mongolia also boasts a large number of warm springs and mineral water, mainly in the east area, including the warm springs in the Jalai Nur of Manzhouli, Arxan in Hinggan League, Aohan of Chifeng, Ningcheng, Hexigten Banner and Liangcheng Daihai of Ulanqab and Weinahe mineral water in the Ewenki Autonomous Banner of Hulun Buir League. The warm spring and mineral water contain many minerals beneficial to human bodies, and can treat many diseases. Most of them are famous summer resort.

Places of Intrests With Mongolian Characteristics

The cultural tour of the Inner Mongolia has Mongolian characteristics. The places of interests in the region can be divided into four categories: The ancient tombs, ancient city ruins, temples and pagodas and cultural ruins.

Ancient tombs. They include Cemetery of Genghis Khan, Tomb of Wang Zhaojun (Wang Qiang), Cemetery of Liaotaizu, Qing Cemetery of the Liao Dynasty, Tomb of Lady Min of the Eastern Han Dynasty, group tombs of Xianbei ethnic group in Jalai Nur, group tombs of Jalai Nur, group tombs of the Liao Dynasty, stone coffin tomb of the local official of Lingzhou and the Han Tomb in Helinge'er. Of them, the Cemetery of Genghis Khan and Tomb of Wang Zhaojun are the most typical ones.

Visitors from both home and abroad, when stepping onto the great land of Inner Mongolia, can't help thinking of Genghis Khan, proud son of Heaven for his time. The cemetery is located in the Ejin Horo Banner of the Ih Ju League, 65 km from Dongsheng. It covers an area of 55,544 square meters and is composed of three Mongolian yurts inlaid with colorful glazed tiles. The main building is composed of a doorway copying the style of the gateway of the Yuan Dynasty and three Mongolian yurts

Dinosaur fossil, with a history of 120 million years, was found in Jalai Nur in Hulun Buir League connected with each other, which is divided into the main hall, east and west wing halls, east and west corridors and back hall. The whole building looks imposing.

A 5-meter-high white marble sculpture of Genghis Khan sits in the center of the main hall, with a huge map as a background and an incense burner in front of it. The light goes on forever. Behind the yellow curtain of the back hall are enshrined coffins of Genghis Khan and his wife, and behind the yellow curtains on its both sides are coffins of the second and third wives of Genghis Khan and those of his two brothers. In the east hall are the coffins of his fourth son Tuolei and the latter's wife, and in the west hall are nine spear-like weapons representing the nine generals of Genghis Khan as well as the knife and horse whip once used by him. Paintings depicting great events in Genghis Khan's life can be seen on the walls of the two corridors.

1,000-year Chinese pine

There are many stories about the mausoleum. One goes that about 700 years ago, Genghis Khan led his troops on a west expedition. When he passed the Erdos Plateau, he was intoxicated by the beautiful scene. Dropping his horse whip, he sat on his horse, meditating. He regarded the site as a place for a declining dynasty to revive, for common people to live in, for spotted deer to grow and for the aged to rest. He also asked his descendants to bury him there upon his death. According to historians and archaeologists, Ejin Horo means "mausoleum of the master". On March 21,

May 15,　September 12 and October 3 each year according to China's lunar calendar,　the descendants of Genghis Khan will hole grand sacrificing activities here.　Also,　horse banquet and Erdos marrying ceremonies will be staged here irregularly.

The old story of Wang Zhaojun was passed down to later generations by poems,　operas and folk stories,　which often arouse people's desire to see her tomb.

Many visitors to Hohhot will go to see the Tomb of Wang Zhaojun, which is situated 9 km away from the capital city of Inner Mongolia.　The tomb is actually an earth hill,　measuring 33 meters high.　In 33 AD during the reign of the Yuan Emperor during the Han Dynasty,　Wang Zhaojun,　a beauty then,　went to the frontier areas to marry Chan Yu,　the chieftain of Xiongnu,　a tribe in north China.　Since her marriage,　the Han and Xiongnu live in harmony for more than 60 years.　It is said that every autumn when grass and trees become dry,　the tomb is still covered with greenness,　so it is also called "Qingzhong"　(meaning green tomb).　Wang Zhaojun has become an envoy for peace and friendship in people's minds,　and is therefore respected by people of all generations.

Mongolian-way wrestling

Scenic Spots and Folk Customs

The 200-year-old Wudang Monastery--one of the three Tibetan Buddhism monasteries of China

Ancient City Ruins. In Inner Mongolia, such ruins can be found as the Yunzhong City (City in the Cloud) of the Zhao and Qin states during the Warring States Period (BC457-BC221), Guanglusai Ruins of the Western Han Dynasty (BC206-25AD), Machi Ancient City Ruins and Chifeng Heicheng Ruins of the Han Dynasty (BC206-220AD), Ruins of Tongwan City, former capital of Daxia Kingdom of the Jin Dynasty (265-420), Shi'erliancheng Ruins of the Sui Dynasty (581-618), Sanshouxiangcheng Ruins and Chan Yu Dadu Ruins of the Tang Dynasty, Zuzhou, Shangjing, Zhongjing and Qingzhou ruins of the Liao Dynasty (916-1125), Halahot and Jinsilangcheng ancient city ruins, Shangdu and Yingchanglu ruins of the Yuan Dynasty (1279-1368) and Princess's Residence of the Qing Dynasty (1644-1911).

The Shangdu city, an imposing ancient city of the Yuan Dynasty, is found in the deep grasses of Zhenglan Banner in the Xilin Gol Grassland. This was the capital decided by Kublai Khan (grandson of Genghis Khan)

when he ascended to the Khan position of Inner Mongolia. Shangdu city is the political, economic, military and cultural center at the beginning of the Yuan Dynasty. Historical records show that the Shangdu city once extended to the desert in the north and Beijing in the south. As 700 years have passed, its prosperity no longer exists. However, while strolling in the ancient ruins, people can still imagine the high buildings and residence structure of the past.

Temples and pagodas. There are Zhenji Temple in the Liao grottoes, Wuta, Dazhao, Xiaozhao, Xilitu, Wusutu, Wudang, Meidai, Junggar, Qang'ai, Bailing, Xingyuan, Genghis Khan, Agui, Beizi, Gegen, Yanfu, Lama Cave, Kundulun, Meiligeng, Baotou, Huifu temples and monasteries, Hohhot Mosque, Daming Pagoda, White Tower and Sakyamuni Pagoda. Of these, the Wudang Monastery enjoys the same reputation as that of Potala Palace of Tibet and Ta'er Temple of Qinghai. They are the three famous temples of Lamaism in China.

The Wudang Monastery is situated in deep mountains along brooks. Pines and simmering water surround the holy land of Lamaism. This is where Mongolian herdsmen offer their sacrifices and a tourism attraction.

Wudang Monastery is the largest and most complete Tibetan Lamasery in Inner Mongolia. Situated in the Wudang gully of Yinshan Mountains, it is 70 km northwest to Baotou. The Wudang Monastery has three different names. In Mongolian, it means "willow", representing the luxuriant willows in the valley in front of the temple. In Tibetan, it means "white lotus" and in Chinese, it is called "Guangjue Temple, " granted by Emperor Qianlong in 1756.

Wudang Monastery was built during the reign of Kangxi in the Qing Dynasty. Imitating the Zhaxi Lhumbo Monastery of Tibet, the Wudang Monastery was renovated several times during the Qianlong, Jiaqing and Guangxu reigns before it reached the present scale. There are altogether 2,538 halls and houses, covering about 200,000 square meters. In the golden time, it houses 1,200 lamas. All buildings feature Tibetan styles: Flat top, vertical wall, little window and white color. Sitting against the pines and cypresses in the mountains, it looks very grand. The whole building is composed of six halls, three residences, one main room and 94 residential buildings for lamas. Statistics show there are more than 1,500 Buddha sculptures made of gold, silver, bronze, wood and earth. The largest one is as tall as a three-story building and the tiniest one is no higher than 3 cm. The large number of murals in the monastery vividly depict historical figures, folk customs, legends, mountains and rivers and flowers and birds. They are precious materials for the study of the history and culture of minority ethnic groups in China.

Now, the Wudang Monastery is still a place for lamas to hold Buddhist activities and for Buddhism followers to worship. Each year, there will be meetings of lamas and nuns.

Cultural ruins. Located in the northern border of China, Inner Mongolia boasts many ethnic groups and a long history and colorful culture.

Hometown of dinosaurs. Erenhot of Xilin Gol League is a birthplace of dinosaur fossils which was first recorded into the international history of ancient extinct lives. In about 70 million years ago, Yanchi area of Erenhot was covered with lakes and marshlands, with humid and hot climate and luxuriant forests, which is a paradise for dinosaurs. Since the 1890s, paleontologists and geologists from Russia, the United States and China have conducted six large-scale investigations and excavations and found fossils of more than 10 species of dinosaurs. Many relatively complete dinosaur fossils have been unearthed here, and the discovery of dinosaur eggs is the earliest in China.

In October 1989, a Dinosaur Museum was set up in Erenhot. What on display are vivid and grandeur dinosaurs, which have attracted tens of thousands of visitors from home and abroad.

Yinshan cliff paintings. In the Yinshan Mountains of Bayan Nur League, about 10,000 cliff paintings have been discovered. They are precious treasures in ancient art treasure house of the Chinese nation. Most are paintings about animals, and some are about hunting. Some paintings represent the activities and lives of herdsmen in the north. Besides, there are also scenes of herding, dancing, vehicles, warriors and warriors' troops, people's faces, hand and foot marks, bird and beast foot marks and cultural activities. Also, some reflect the primitive religious figures and totems.

As cultural relics in north grassland, the Yinshan cliff paintings demonstrate the wisdom and creativity of northern nomadic.

Hongshan Culture. Hongshan, situated 3 km northeast of Chifeng, is famous across the world because of its culture featuring the Neolithic Age.

Hongshan Mountain is 665 meters above the sea level, covering an area of 670 hectares. The entire mountain is made up of red granites. Seen from the due north, the five peaks of the Hongshan Mountain look like five lotuses.

Camel racing

Between them four saddle-shaped areas have been formed. Under the sunlight, the whole mountain is red, like burnt clouds. Climbing from the first saddle, people will find a gray granite like an inscribed board inlaid in the naked mountain, which is known as "Muzhi Tablet. " There are two caves nearby, called "Gezitang" (Pigeons' Hall). In front of the caves is a huge stone as smooth as a mirror. If you come to the top of the mountain, you will see a section of Great Wall ruins left over from the Spring and Autumn period (about 9 century BC).

The Neolithic Age site was discovered in the southern side and back slope of the Hongshan Mountain, which forms the "Hongshan Culture. " Now the Hongshan Mountain has been developed into a scenic spot.

In Inner Mongolia, people will also see the largest stoneware manufacturing field with the most deposits and dating back earliest as well as the mysterious Heicheng city.

An Ethnic Group on Horse's Back

Inner Mongolia Autonomous Region is home to 49 ethnic groups including Mongolian, Han, Man, Hui, Daur, Ewenki and Oroqen. Due to the differences in living environment, producing and living conditions and development process, each ethnic group has formed its own customs.

Mongolian. This is the main ethnic group in Inner Mongolia. In history, it lives on husbandry, therefore, its culture is about horses.

Traditional virtues. In the mind of Mongolians, the white color represents holiness, nobility and auspiciousness and the number "nine" symbolizes holiness and abundance. They think the "right" is to be respected, while the "left" means humility.

The Mongolians are hospitable and sincere. When they first meet guests, they will say hello to them. Once the guests step into their yurts, the hostess will present to them the milk tea as well as butter, milk skin, milk bean curd, cheese and milk wine. To the distinguished guests, the hada will be presented to show their respect.   The accommodation and food are free of charge.   As the guests are to leave,   the whole family will come out and give them the best wishes.

Mongolian yurts.   Mongolian yurts are traditional residences of the ethnic group.   They are the result of the nomadic life the Mongolians lived in the past.   Now most of the Mongolians have settled down.   The yurts are a kind of tent pitched by wool felts.   Scattering on the vast grassland,   they look like white lotuses.   In the middle of the yurt's top,   there are windows to give out smoke and let in the air and light.   Usually a wooden frame door will be opened to the south or southeast.   People feel warm in winter and cool in summer living in the yurts.   Also,   the yurts are easily to dissemble and install and transport.

Milk tea,   delicious wine and meat.   The foods of Mongolians are divided into three kinds: the milk,   meat and grain.   The milk food include

Horse racing

Wedding ceremony of Mongolians

the white butter, yellow butter, milk skin, milk bean curd, cheese and milk fruits, while the milk beverage include milk tea, sour milk and milk wine.

The meat and milk are the essential materials to Mongolians. They have great breakfast and dinner. In the morning, they like drink milk tea and eat millet stir-fried in butter as well as some milk skin and milk bean curd. In the evening, they will eat noodles boiled in mutton soup, fresh milk cake or mutton. Any time of the day, they can drink the milk tea if they like.

The meat is mainly mutton and beef. As to mutton, they will boil or roast it. They often select fat and tender sheep and boil it to 70 or 80 percent cooked. Then they can hold it or cut it to pieces before eating. The mutton tastes very good. The roasted whole sheep is a special dish of the Mongolian ethnic group. The sheep is wholly roasted until it becomes brown. The chef then will take it to guests and cut it into patches and pieces. The color, fragrance, taste and form all looks fine. There are also hot pot mutton. It is said that after one severe fight in

Splendid attire of Mongolian girls

south expedition, Kublai Khan and his troops felt very tired and hungry. Just as they were slaughtering sheep to prepare food, they got the message that enemies were only five km away. Kublai Khan immediately gave the order to start while calling "Mutton, mutton!" The chefs suddenly thought out a way. They quickly sliced the sheep into pieces and put them into the boiled water. When the mutton changed color, they put in some salt, onion and ginger pieces and handed it to Kublai. Kublai got a great victory. When celebrating the success, Kublai thought of the sliced mutton. So the chefs made it in a more delicate way and put in more sauces as fermented bean curd and pepper oil. Kublai named it as "hot pot mutton", which spread to many other places later. The mutton of Donglaishun Restaurant in Beijing today still attracts visitors from home and abroad.

The beef can also be boiled or roasted to eat.

Beautiful clothes. The plateau, grassland, desert and the unpredictable weather have cultivated the clothes and ornaments of Mongolian people: The jewelry, long gown, belt and boot.

Women have to wear jewelry when visiting relatives and friends on holidays. The jewelry is made from different materials such as agate, pearl,

Offering sacrifices at aobao

Mongolian boots

Hair ornaments of Mongolians

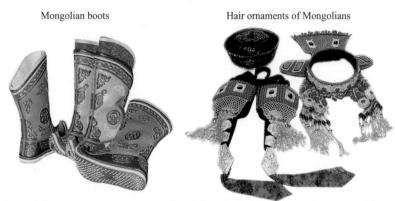

coral, jadeite, precious stones and gold and silver wares and arranged into different designs. The most typical one is the head jewelry of Erdos, which select finesse materials and weighs 15-20 kg.

Men and women, the old or children, all like wear long gowns on festivals or important meetings. This is a traditional clothes made during the long nomadic life. The long gown is broad, with no slit on either side. It has long sleeves and high collar. The buttons are on the right. The neckband, wristband and the gown hem are all trimmed with laces. The gown for men are usually blue or brown, while that for women are red, green and purple. In different seasons, they wear gowns of different thickness, the single-layered one, the double-layered one, the cotton-layered one and the feather one. Belt, cap and riding boots are necessary for those dressed in long gowns. Men will put the gown hem up to make themselves look strong, while women like to pull the gown hem down to show their posture.

The Mongolian boots are made of cloth, feather or felt. The cloth boots are usually made from high-class cloth, trimmed with golden silk laces on its face, and the design with strong local flavor. They look special and feel soft. The feather boots are made from cattle skin, divided into old and new styles. The old style ones are made from unsmooth cattle skin, looking very clumsy. The leg part is over 30 cm and the sole is of multiple layers. It looks like a boat in the whole. The new style ones, made from smooth cattle skin, are solid and durable. The felt boots are mould pressed from sheep or cattle wool. The herdsmen have to wear them to go through the severe winter. The Mongolian boots are all broad so that felt to protect leg, cotton socks and foot wrapping could be used. As a result, the Mongolians protect their feet and legs well in icy winter even if they go across rivers or deep snow.

Special wedding ceremony. The wedding ceremony of Mongolians is very grand and solemn though in different characteristics. In pastoral areas, the bride and bridegroom will have to circle the Mongolian yurts three times before they get off cars or horses. Then they must go through the roaring fire to show the purity and faithfulness of their love and prosperity of their new life. Once they go into the yurts, they first prostrate themselves before the image of Buddha, then they meet parents and relatives. After that, they will change the style of hair and clothes. A whole sheep banquet will be presented and milk food and candies are found everywhere. People will spend the whole night celebrating by presenting a hada and wine, singing and dancing. Of all kinds of wedding ceremonies, those of Urad and Erdos are the most famous.

Grand and solemn sacrificial rites. The most popular and grand sacrificial rite is offered to aobao. The aobao is usually a cone-shaped pagoda piled up with stones on high mountains or small hills. On top of it is planted a long pole, fastened with wool or horn of animals and cloth stripes with s c r i p t u r e s . Surrounding it are stones on which

Mongolian knife

147

incenses are burnt. The sacrifices are often made during June, July and August when grass is lush and animals fatty. At the time, men and women, the old and children, all come to the place with hadas, whole roasted sheep, milk wine and milk foods. After they present their hadas and sacrifices, lamas will chant the scriptures. Then the people will add stones or willow branches to aobao. Also, new colorful stripes and Buddhist sutra will be put on. After the sacrificial rite, entertainment activities such as the horse-racing, wrestling and archery will be held, which was later developed into Nadam Fair.

Nadam Fair. In the Mongolian language, Nadam means recreation or entertainment. The Nadam Fair is a traditional gathering now celebrated once each year. It started in 1225 when Genghis Khan wanted to celebrate a victory. In ancient times, the festival involved three basic skills of combat-horse racing, archery and wrestling. Although these events have survived

Dating at the aobao fair

Mongolian girls of Buliyate

to modern times, other events have been added, such as reading, singing, dancing, chess, polo, marksmanship and track and field competitions. The Nadam Fair has grown into a mass gathering involving both genders. During the festivities, young men and women also get the chance to meet and talk of love and marriage. The fathering also attracts merchants, artists, business exhibitors and tourists.

Nadam is usually held in mid-summer. During several days of festivities, Mongolian herders will gather from surrounding areas. Wearing traditional garb, they will take part in competitions or simply play the role of spectators. Many companies will set up exhibition tents or sales booths. Cultural troupes, film crews and science and technology exhibitors will also join the activities.

During the mid-summer months of July and August, the vast grasslands of Inner Mongolia become a sea of songs and flowers. Through Nadam people celebrate a good harvest and eulogize a happy life. Hospitable representatives of various ethnic groups of the Inner Mongolia Autonomous Region take advantages of the opportunities during the Nadam Fair to welcome friends from around the world.

Hometown of songs and dances. Known as "hometown of songs"

and "sea of dances, " Inner Mongolia has a long history of culture and art, which is a great part of the Chinese culture and art. The famous literary works include *Secret History of Inner Mongolia*, *Jiangger* and *Gesi'er*. And there are also songs and dances, musical instruments and paintings.

Jiangger is a grand folk epic. It is one of the three greatest epics of China, with another two as *King Gesar* of Tibetans and *Manasi* of Kirgiz. In the past 200 years, the collection and study on *Jiangger* is going on, which has now developed into an independent academic subject of the world.

Mongolian folk songs are often heard in pastoral areas. They are divided into long and short tunes. The long tune songs have few words, stressing the vastness and broad mind of Mongolians. The short tune songs are in strict rhythms. Both demonstrate the simplicity, hospitality and boldness of Mongolians.

Attire of Daur ethnic group

Haolaibao is a popular singing method in Inner Mongolia. It has fixed tunes, while the words are often improvisations. It is usually in antiphonal style. Sometimes, one sings, the other answers or the others answer. Sometimes, it becomes chorus.

Mongolian dances include the horse and knife dance, Erdos dance, chopsticks dance or bowl dance. The rhythm is lively and dancing steps brisk, representing the simplicity, enthusiasm and straightforwardness of the ethnic group.

Matouqin (a bowed stringed instrument with a scroll carved like a horse's head) is a special musical instrument with Mongolians. The player sings accompanying his tune, which is very attractive.

All other ethnic groups on this vast land have their own characteristics. We mainly introduce the folk customs of Daur, Ewenki and Oroqen.

Daur Ethnic Group. The ethnic group lives in Hulun Buir League, who sets up the Daur Autonomous Banner of Morin Dawa.

Building features. Daur villages are often found in places facing water and against mountains. The houses and courtyards are often fenced with red willow, birch or oak branches. With the ridges sticking out, they all look like a Chinese character "*jie*", so people call them "*jie* character houses. " In the tradition of Daur, they give much respect to the west, so people live in west houses and beds built in south, west and north sides.

Wedding ceremony. After a boy and a girl is engaged, the man will select a fine day to send betrothal gifts to the girl's. The first one is called "*cha'ente*", including five pigs, one horse, one cow as well as white spirit, cakes and milk skin. The second one is called "*tuolie*", in which the cloth, clothes and jewelry will be presented. One month before the marriage, the boy has to send small gifts to the girl's and have "*lali millet*". At the wedding ceremony, an aged will hold an arrow while giving congratulatory speeches. The speeches are often about the mutual respect and love between the couple, wishing the bride to give respect to the aged and love for the children, and hoping the bridegroom to come back with full carriages with an arrow going out.

Clothes and jewelry. The boots the Daur

Attire of Ewenki ethnic group

151

wears in winter are usually made of dog skin with furs outside and the soles are made from roe deer or cattle skins, called "*qikami*" and "*tatemale*" respectively. The roe deer skin gown by Daur men in spring and autumn goes down to knees, with slit left in the front, and the gown in winter is even longer, with bronze buttons or buttons knitted with cloth stripes. The herdsmen wear long gowns made from roe deer with furs out and hats made from roe deer, wolf or fox skins. The Daur women like embroidery. They trim the clothes hems, wrist and neck bands with laces. Girls on their wedding ceremony must put on the clogs with embroidered silk on the uppers.

Ewenki Ethnic Group. Ewenki means "people living among mountains" in their own language.

Geibu. This means "family tree" in Ewenki language. A clan meeting will be held every 20 years. The head will write down the names of female members of the same surname. The family tree book is kept by clan head and cannot be opened freely. Each Spring Festival according to China's lunar calendar, all clan members will kowtow and offer spirit to the family tree to show their respect to the ancestors.

Residence. Ewenki people live in a round tent, called "xianrenzhu" (meaning immortal's pillar). The tent is put up with birch or willow trunks and branches. In summer and autumn, it is covered with hay, reed or birch tree skin; while in winter, it is coated with beasts' skins. The gate usually faces east or south. The tents have to be arranged in a line or circle, but not in front and back rows.

Jinle. This means skiing slate in Ewenki language. It is made from pine wood, with its front bending upward and the back like a slope. In the middle of it is a rope to tie foot. The Ewenki people use it as a transportation tool in hunting.

Talajiabi. This is a special water transportation tool of Ewenki people. It looks like a boat. The boat body is made from birch wood and the whole boat is wrapped with birch bark. They are knitted together with red pine roots. The needle holes will be filled with a kind of mixed black oil decocted from pine rosin and birch bark. The boat is six meters long, 1.5 meters high and 0.6 meters wide. With both ends bending upwards, the boat can travel at a speed of 20km/hour.

Zandalaga. This is a general term of folk songs of Ewenki. The short one is only several lines while the long one will go to dozens of lines. Some are passed down from former generations while others are created impromptus. The melody is simple, with no instrumental accompany.

Gaolebukan dance. This is bonfire dance, popular in Ewenki in Aolu Guya of Genhe city. In wedding ceremony or gathering of two clans, people will sing and dance at the riverside. Seven to 20 people, hand in hand, will form a circle. They move in the direction the sun moves.

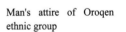

Man's attire of Oroqen ethnic group

Aidaha pas de deux. This is a kind of dance for two persons, who imitate the fighting between two wild roars.

Hongge. This is a song sung by Ewenki people when they find the mother cattle and sheep do not recognize the calf or lamb.

Oroqen Ethnic Group. Oroqen is one of the ethnic groups with the fewest people in China. In their own language, Oroqen means people living on top of mountains or people taming deer. The Oroqen people in the Oroqen Autonomous Banner of Hulun Buir League to the east of Greater Hinggan Mountains live on hunting. Since 1949, they have dropped their hunting

Foreign visitors on the grassland

guns and engaged themselves in modern industries. In 1996, the autonomous banner issued a notice forbidding hunting in this area, a historic step forward to modernization.

Residence. The Oroqen people live in houses called "chulun angga" or "xierenzhu. "

Birch bark facilities. The Oroqen people keep well the birch culture in north China. Their daily utensils, including ashen (bowl), ahan (basin), mulingkaiyi (wooden barrel), kunji (basket), aosha (sewing box), adamala (box) and tiekesha (defensive wall of the house) are all made from birches. On these things are often painted colorful designs.

People on the vast land of Inner Mongolia sing such songs to show their real life, "My home is on the beautiful grassland, with countless flowers when blows the wind. Butterflies go through them and birds sing, with a green water reflecting the setting sun. Steed runs like clouds and cattle and sheep are scattered on the land like pearls....... "

154

Appendix

Appendix I. Preferential Policies Encouraging Foreign Investment in Inner Mongolia Autonomous Region

Article 1. The regulations are drafted with the aim of further absorbing foreign investment and accelerating the development of an export-oriented economy of the autonomous region.

Article 2. The regulations are applicable to companies, enterprises, economic organizations or individuals of foreign countries, Hong Kong, Macao and Taiwan, which establish Sino-foreign joint ventures, foreign-invested enterprises and solely-foreign funded enterprises (hereinafter referred to as foreign-funded enterprises) and other public facilities in the autonomous region.

Article 3. Foreign-funded productive enterprises scheduled to operate for a period of 10 years, after the approval from local taxation departments, can get back the income tax five years after they begin making profits. Local authorities can keep 25 percent of the value added tax (VAT) and return it to enterprises after five years of operation. Industrial items encouraged to develop in the autonomous region will be issued by local trade and economic committee together with other relevant departments. For enterprises in operation for no more than 10 years, the returned income tax and VAT should be pursued.

Article 4. Foreign-funded enterprises with high investment are encouraged.

(1) Productive foreign-funded enterprises and high-tech enterprises set up in capital cities, coastal cities and high-tech development zones approved by the State Council enjoy preferential taxation policies as coastal (or border) open cities and high-tech zones.

(2) Foreign-funded enterprises with over US$5 million of foreign investment and scheduled to operate for a period of 10 years or more and those engaged in service trades shall pay income tax according to the set rate starting from the profit-making year. Fifty percent of their payments shall later be refunded by local financial authorities.

Article 5. High-tech enterprises and export-oriented enterprises in development zones shall pay income tax according to the rate set by the state. The amount surpassing 15 percent shall be refunded by local financial authorities.

Article 6. Foreign investors, if use their profits to reinvest in new export-oriented enterprises or expand export-oriented enterprises, with a operation period of no less than five years, shall be refunded the business income taxes in the reinvestment, upon examination and approval by local financial authorities. If their products are provided for export, they shall apply to the exemption (or reduction) tax policy carried out by the state now. If the output value of products for export exceeds 60 percent of the year's total output value of the enterprises, the income tax surpassing 10 percent shall be refunded to enterprises by local financial authorities after examination and approval.

Article 7. All foreign-funded enterprises are exempted from local income tax.

Article 8. Foreign investors, who invest in energy, transportation or other infrastructure projects, are encouraged to conduct construction and operation in forms of build-operate-transfer (BOT), project financing and operation right transfer. Those investing in key transportation projects and old urban area renovation, upon approval, can expand its operation to land development and services in surrounding areas. The enterprises upon the approval of the autonomous regional financial and price authorities may decide price and charge.

Foreign investors are further encouraged to invest in high-grade road construction. The business tax on vehicle passage will all be refunded to enterprises by the local financial authorities in the first eight years of traffic opening.

Article 9. Foreign investors are allowed to obtain the overall or part of property rights of state-owned enterprises at the county or banner level or above upon approval the people's government by way of purchasing, shareholding, majority share holding and assuming debts.

Article 10. Preferential policies shall be implemented for land use.

(1) Foreign-funded enterprises are exempted from land use fees within the ratified construction period;

(2) Foreign investors, who run enterprises on available land and have a contract to operate for a period of 10 years or more shall be exempted from land sue fees for the first five years of operation.

(3) With regard to export enterprises, high-tech enterprises and foreign-funded enterprises engaged in energy, transportation, infrastructure construction, resources development and raw material production, whose operation period is 15 years or more, land use fees shall be exempted in the first five years of operation for those with investments of US$500,000 to US$ 1 million. The exemption shall last seven years for those with investments of US$1.01 million to US$ 3 million, 10 years for those with investments of US$3.01-5 million and 15 years for those with investments of more than US $5 million.

(4) Foreign-funded enterprises if want to improve the degenerated grassland of pastoral areas, after obtaining the land use right by law, shall develop according to the regulations of the autonomous region.

(5) Foreign-funded enterprises devoted to planting and raising industries, upon approval of the people's government, can get a land use right of 50 years.

(6) Priority will be given to foreign investors who want to develop wild mountains, land, desert, beach and gully into farming land. With approval from the government with such right, the developer can have a land use right for 50 years. If they are developed for other construction purposes, after the certain scale is reached according to contract, the proportion in land sue fee kept by local authorities shall be all refunded to enterprises.

(7) Foreign investors enjoy due preferential policies with approval from the local government when they are constructing or renovating small towns.

Article 11. Border and remote areas are allowed to submit application to introduce foreign-funded enterprises into their development zones. Relevant departments shall provide conveniences to them in setting up the project, examination and approval, development and tax transfer.

Article 12. With the examination and approval of banks, foreign-funded enterprises shall be given priority to get short-term circulating capital and other necessary loans required during their production and circulation. Approved enterprises may mortgage fixed assets or other properties regulated by the state, or spot exchange, to banks for RMB loans.

Article 13. Foreign-funded enterprises shall be treated as Chinese ones in local fee charging and RMB can be used in settling accounts. Foreign-funded enterprises and the public welfare establishments they run shall have priority in the supply of water, electricity, gas and communication facilities according to their need. A unified charging standard will be followed in foreign-funded and non-foreign-funded enterprises.

Article 14. The urban infrastructure coordination fee shall be reduced by 50 percent for export-oriented enterprises, high-tech enterprises and enterprises involved in energy, transportation, infrastructure construction and raw material production.

Article 15. With regard to the transportation of products, the foreign-funded enterprises shall submit plans to the related transportation departments. These plans shall be granted priority status.

Article 16. Foreigners working in foreign-funded enterprises in the autonomous region and their family members shall be charged housing, food, transportation and medical care fees equal to Chinese residents.

Article 17. The board of directors of foreign-funded enterprises shall, according to related state regulations, independently decide on the standards of salary and bonus and gross pay roll and file them with labor authorities for record. Employees are hired independently by the enterprises. The employees shall go through related procedures with the local labor departments.

Article 18. Foreign-funded enterprises shall enjoy the same preferential policies of the state and the autonomous region in arranging laid-off workers from state-owned enterprises.

Article 19.   Relevant departments must respond within 10 days to application submitted by foreign investors.   If all materials are provided, the business invitation center and project approval center of the autonomous region and relevant leagues will organize and coordinate the commercial, tax environment protection, urban construction, land, foreign trade, financial and planning departments to grant approval for the registration at the quickest speed.

Article 20.   Foreign-funded enterprises are protected by law.   Relevant departments shall strictly follow these rules:

(1) Examination and fine not abiding by laws, rules and regulations are not allowed in foreign-funded enterprises;

(2) Except for the institutions, which can conduct forcible execution according to law and rules and regulations, nobody is allowed to appropriate or frozen the capital and account of foreign-funded enterprises and foreign investors.   Now is he allowed to close down the legal property of them;

(3) Legal rights and interests of foreign-funded enterprises shall not be destroyed.

Article 21.   These regulations take priority over any previously promulgated regulations.

Article 22.   The right to interpret these regulations resides in the Office for Opening-up Affairs under the People's Government of Inner Mongolia Autonomous Region.   The regulations will be implemented on the day they are issued.

Appendix II. Preferential Policies for Further Expansion of Lateral Economic Cooperation

Article 1.   The resources and industries of the Inner Mongolia Autonomous Region, excluding those subject to special state regulations, are open to the whole country. Enterprises of all kinds of ownership, individuals and institutions (hereinafter collectively referred to as "external investors") are encouraged to develop agriculture, animal husbandry, forestry, water and mineral resources, open raw material processing and high-tech industries, conduct integrity between enterprises, participate in the development of energy, transportation, information and construction of infrastructure, old urban area renovation and real estate and develop border trade, tourism, culture, education, public health, sports and all sorts of public welfare undertakings in Inner Mongolia.

Article 2.   The Inner Mongolia Autonomous region opens its market to the whole nation.

(1)   External investors are encouraged to take part in the construction of commodity, technology and labor markets and tourism and recreational arenas. All market commodities are subject to free trade, except those clearly prohibited by state regulations.

(2)   Ministries and commissions under the State Council and various provinces, autonomous regions and municipalities directly under the central government are welcomed to set up representative offices and agencies in the autonomous region. Governments at all levels and relevant departments shall provide them with conveniences.

Article 3.   External investors are welcomed to set up solely-funded, joint-invested or cooperatively operated enterprises in this region, set up branches or sub-companies, or compose trans-regional or trans-industrial conglomerates or enterprise groups.

Article 4.   External investors are welcomed to become shareholders in the region by contributing capital, technology, patents, equipment, administration or famous trade marks, and lease or contract existing enterprises, or jointly run them by administering certain departments or workshops.   They are also welcomed to transfer scientific achievements, highly energy consuming or labor-intensive industries to the region, and cooperate in a broad range including the aspects of processing with materials and according samples supplied by customers, compensation trade, technology and talents.

Article 5.   External investors are welcomed to own all or part of the property of state-owned enterprises, sold with the approval of the people's government at or above the county level in this region, through purchase, merger, shareholding, majority share holding, assumed liability or any other means agreed upon by both sides of cooperation.

Article 6.   External investors are welcomed to take part in joint infrastructure construction in port areas and bases of export-oriented production, and jointly develop border trade and foreign economic and technological cooperation.

Article 7.   By whatever means the external investors cooperate with enterprises or institutions of this region (including solely-funded enterprises), they shall be considered internally-cooperative enterprises and enjoy corresponding preferential policies.

Article 8.   External investors may take part in the trade with Russia and the People's Republic of Mongolia by entrusting this region's enterprises as their agents, which have the right to engage in border trade.   Agent fees shall be leveled at the preferential rates. They are also allowed to compose conglomerates with, or act as branches or sub-plants of the region's enterprises that have the right to engage in import and export business and border trade.   This region shall provide positive assistance for those who intend to invest in or set up representative offices in Russia and Mongolia.

Article 9.   Internally-cooperative enterprises, upon the approval by the Ministry of

Agriculture, the State Forestry Administration and Office for Endangered plants, may enjoy corresponding preferential policies in importing such commodities as seeds and seedlings to develop export farm product.

Article 10. Raw and auxiliary materials, spare parts, components and parts and packing materials that are imported for the production of export products by internally-cooperative enterprises shall apply to the customs for setting up the file of processing trade contract. And the customs will administrate according to relevant rules of processing trade.

Article 11. The provinces, autonomous regions and municipalities, that conduct engineering project contracting and labor cooperation with Russia and Mongolia, shall be exempted from import duties on part of the imported compensation commodities (excluding those prohibited by the state). The remainder shall be considered as border import commodities and enjoy the corresponding preferential policies. The commodities may be resold by importers themselves.

Article 12. Internally-cooperative enterprises funded by external investors shall enjoy a three-year business income tax exemption from the first day of profit-making. A 50 percent reduction in income tax may be allowed for another two years following the expiration of the period for exemptions. The enterprises that invest in industries encouraged by the autonomous region, checked by local tax departments, shall enjoy a five-year period of business income tax exemption from the first day of profit-making. The proportion of VAT kept by local government will be refunded by 50 percent after three years of operation. Enterprises set up in poverty-stricken areas at the state or autonomous regional level shall enjoy a five-year period of business income tax exemption from the first day of operations. The 25 percent of VAT kept by local governments will be all refunded within three years. The item categories encouraged by the autonomous region will be issued by trade and economic committee of the region and relevant departments.

Article 13. As for joint projects aimed at transforming the region's loss-making enterprises, the enterprises are allowed to make up losses with realized profits and shall be exempted from business income tax for another three year after the losses.

Article 14. The income gained by the scientific units and institutions of higher learning from technical services, including transfer of scientific achievements, technical training, technical advice and technical contract shall be exempted from operation tax and income tax.

Internally-cooperative enterprises engaged in technological activities mentioned above enjoy the same preferential policies.

Article 15. Joint ventures and solely-funded enterprises, if they are engaged in tourism, education, culture, transportation industries or transfer of intangible asset or sales of immovable property and local financial industries with certain capital operation field and at a certain scale (with a fixed asset of over 2 million yuan), shall enjoy a preferential policy of refunding 50 percent of its operation tax kept by local governments within five years.

Article 16. Solely-funded, joint or cooperative high-tech enterprises newly set up in the state- or autonomous-region designated development zones shall enjoy the preferential policies in tax as mentioned above. After the period, they shall be levied the income tax at a reduced 15 percent rate.

Article 17. External investors are encouraged to come to this region for development and opening on large tracts of land.

(1) This region shall enable investors to obtain the right to use land by sale, lease and appropriation. The terms of land use may be renewed upon approval after expiration.

(2) External investors are encouraged to develop state-owned barren hills, wastelands, desert and deserted valleys and degenerated grassland. Priority will be given to those able to be developed into farming land. If degenerated grassland can be improved by planting grass and trees, the development institutions or individuals, upon approval of the people's government, can get the right of land use for 50 years.

Article 18. The income coming from planting and animal raising as part of poverty-relief project in impoverished or border areas or hill, gully and water control project to improve ecological environment shall enjoy a 10-year period of agricultural and husbandry tax exemption. The farm and livestock products shall be exempted from special product tax for five years.

Article 19. Investors who fund high-tech industries, public welfare establishment, energy, transportation, communication facilities and raw material industries shall enjoy a 20 to 30 percent reduction in the purchase price of land use right according to set price of land. Investors who purchase land use right in order to develop agriculture, husbandry, forestry, fishery and other resources on the land shall enjoy a 30 to 50 percent reduction in the purchase price according to set price of land. Investors who run high-tech industries, public welfare establishment, energy, transportation, communication facilities and raw material industries in poverty-stricken areas and border areas shall enjoy a 40 to 60 percent reduction in the purchase price of land use right according to set price of land.

Article 20. External investors who gain the land use right by appropriation shall be exempted from land use fees from the first year of operations. Those who gain the land use right through purchase or lease shall enjoy a 10 percent reduction in the purchase price of land use right or a five-year exemption from rent if the projects are located in economic and technological development zones or experimental zones. If the projects are developed in other areas, they shall enjoy a 5 percent reduction in the purchase price of land use right or a three-year rent exemption following the completion of the said projects.

Article 21. External investors who have gained the land use right and whose volume of investment in development and construction has exceeded 25 percent of the total prescribed in contract, if the land is available for developing industrial production, may according to law transfer, rent and mortgage the land during the term of use or use the land as a condition of joint investment, cooperation or joint operation.

Article 22. The internally-cooperative enterprises jointly established by external investors and this region shall be given priority in the supply of water, electricity, gas and communication facilities required. Internally-cooperative enterprises engaged in construction of energy, transportation and other infrastructure facilities and raw material production shall enjoy a 50 percent reduction in municipal infrastructure coordinating fees.

Article 23. Commercial banks of the autonomous region shall designate a certain size of credit each year in support of lateral economic cooperation. If internally-cooperative enterprises need short-term circulating capital during production and circulation, they shall have precedence in getting loans according to credit issuing procedures after verification by enterprise and internal cooperation responsible departments and approval by banks.

Article 24. Shortages in circulating capital for investment in the state- or regionally-designated old revolutionary, frontier, poverty-stricken and minority inhabited areas may be diverted from local loans earmarked for economic development, poverty relief or other loan programs.

Article 25. Special considerations shall be given to internally-cooperative projects which would produce great influence on regional socio-economic development. Corresponding policies and regulations may be formulated according to the need of the projects.

Article 26. Cooperative enterprises with investment of external investors exceeding 25 percent of total assets shall fully enjoy preferential policies for lateral economic cooperation. If the cooperation is limited to one workshop, a branch factory, or a single project, corresponding preferential policies shall be provided.

Article 27. Procedures governing internal cooperation shall be further simplified. The autonomous region, as well as regional leagues and cities, shall implement a system of streamlined service to solve the problems demanding prompt attention. Responsible departments must respond within 10 days upon receipt of documents to applications submitted by internally-cooperative enterprises. Industrial and commercial administrative departments shall clearly publish all registration procedures and required documents for application as an internally-cooperative enterprise. If all required information is provided, the license shall be granted within 10 days. If the requirements of enterprises comply with laws and regulations, the business invitation center and project examination and approval center of the autonomous region, leagues or cities will coordinate among industrial, commercial, tax, environment protection, land and planning departments to process the procedures.

Article 28. All internally-cooperative enterprises and projects shall report to the local lateral cooperation administration department for record. The department shall cooperate with certain related departments to confirm the form of cooperation, content and investment ratios and then, grant the enterprises a certification as a guarantee of eligibility for preferential policies.

Article 29. The autonomous region shall protect the legal rights and interests of solely- or jointly-funded enterprises involving external investors. The enterprises shall have the autonomy to decide, according to law, on their own modes of operation, labor and salaries, product development, technical improvements, profit distribution and finances.

Article 30. The autonomous region has a service department to handle complaints, coordinate government functions and offer consultation to internally-cooperative enterprises, helping them resolve economic and civil disputes. If mitigation is ineffective, the department shall aid concerned enterprises undergoing audits legal procedures. In case an internal enterprise fails to pay the investor capital or materials as set in cooperative agreement or contract, the department shall be responsible for urging it to pay within a specified time limit. If payment is in arrears, the department shall help the creditor file suit in the people's court for solutions.

Article 31. For those with an investment of 1 million or more yuan in fixed assets, they can settle down in the autonomous region. Their spouses and unmarried children can also come here, free of all kinds of fees. External senior administrative personnel and engineering and technical staff members shall enjoy preferential treatment in terms of salary, housing, schooling and public aid.

Article 32. External investors shall enjoy simultaneous services. Liaison officials will be sent to key investment projects, who are responsible for the handling of relevant problems. The key internally-cooperative enterprises will be particularly protected to prevent from illegal charging, apportion and fine.

Article 33. These regulations take priority over any previously published regulations.

Article 34. The right to interpret these regulations resides in the Office of Opening-up Affairs of the Inner Mongolia Autonomous Region. The regulations shall come into effect from the date of their promulgation.

Appendix III. Opinions of General Offices of Party Committee and People's Government of Inner Mongolia on Further Enhancing the Training, Use and Introduction of Talented People (Revised on April 10, 2000)

To fully implement the strategy of revitalizing the Inner Mongolia Autonomous Region by science and technology, meet the demand in the western development for talents and promote technological innovation and high-tech industrialization, General Offices of Party Committee and People's Government of Inner Mongolia put forward the following opinions on training, use and introduction of talents according to real conditions of the region:

I. Fully realize the significance of talents training, use and introduction from a strategic view and enhance the senses of urgency and responsibility.

1. Since the reform and opening-up, Inner Mongolia Autonomous Region has taken a lot of measures on the training, use and introduction of talents, thus strengthening the talents team and making important contributions to the economic development and social progress of the region. However, the talent team is far from meeting the needs of the region. The little number of talented people, shortage of scientific research leaders, irrational structure of the talent team and outflow of talents have restricted the economic and social development of the region in various degrees, so they must be paid great attention to. In the 21st century, science and technology develop rapidly, economic development will depend much on scientific progress and technological innovation as well as the development of market economy and economic globalization. Therefore, we will succeed only when we possess advantages in talents. Party committees and governments at all levels should play scientific progress at a key position in line with the requirements put forward in the 15th Congress of Communist Party of China and take more positive measures to grasp the training, use and introduction of talents.

II. Find focuses of the work and try to set up a high-quality talent team as soon as possible.

2. According to the actual need of technological innovation in pillar industries of the region and industrialization development of high technology, Inner Mongolia will select a group of academic leaders with internationally advanced levels and a group of young talents with technologies advanced in China or abroad and give them special funds and training. Enterprises and institutions should select young professional technicians and send them to universities or colleges within or out of the region to receive further education. Enterprises and institutions are encouraged to send key technical members to study abroad.

Relevant departments of the autonomous region should further enhance the work of sending students abroad on public funds.

3. The scientific commission, planning commission and education departments should appropriate a certain sum of money each year in the establishment and improvement of key

subjects and key laboratories in the autonomous region. On the basis of the present universities able to confer doctor's or master's degrees, the Inner Mongolia will increase the university enrollment rate and improve training qualities. In large-scale enterprises, the laboratory for post-doctoral pursuers will be established to promote the combination of production, study and research. Also, new ways will be explored in training postgraduates, Ph. D.s or above for certain enterprises. Enterprises and scientific institutions are encouraged to set up fellowship or assistantship in subjects they need or to excellent students. Graduates then will come to the autonomous region to work.

III. Expand channels, create conditions and actively introduce talents from home and abroad.

4. High-level talents will be introduced into the region according to the need of economic and social development. The major objects are academician of Chinese Academy of Sciences (CAS) and Chinese Academy of Engineering (CAE) and postgraduates and Ph. Ds of the two institutions, professional technicians urgently needed in the scientific and economic development of the region, leaders of high-tech industries, key projects and new subjects, professionals with individual invention, patent or technological achievement and high-level operation and management talents.

5. Different ways will be taken in attracting talents. Talents can work in the autonomous region for a long time, or just be hired, or just participate in shares and contracts, or give lectures, provide consultations or transfer technological achievements. Relevant departments of the autonomous region should regularly organize enterprises, institutions of higher learning and scientific institutions and bring their project or subject to other places of China or even foreign countries to introduce in excellent peoples who can lead an industry, an area, a product or a subject. Talents bases will be set up to publish talents information regularly, thus putting talents onto markets.

IV. Deepen reforms and set up a market mechanism on talents training, use and introduction.

6. Explore new ways of distribution based on knowledge and technology and decide distribution according to market, effectiveness and publicity. Ensure that scientific and technological staff can get a relatively higher income on the basis of their innovative labor. Institutions can transfer the research achievements of their technicians and allocate no less than 20 percent of the net income to the technicians. As for those making economic profits

by their own technology, project and patent, they can get award from government as well as their due pay from the institutions they work for.

7. The policy of giving great award to scientific and technical staff with striking contributions will be continued. Inner Mongolia will give special awards to those having obtained the state first-class or second-class awards in natural sciences, state first-class award in invention, state first-class award in scientific progress and the highest award for excellent teaching at the state level. Those having gotten awards in other classes will also be awarded accordingly.

8. A subsidy system will be set up in special positions as academicians, supervisor of Ph. D. candidates, professionals and technicians with the titles of senior ranks and Ph. D. candidates. The government allots a subsidy of 3,000 yuan per month to academicians of the CAS and CAE, 1,000 yuan to supervisors of Ph. D. candidates, 400 yuan to professionals and technicians with the titles of senior rank and 300 yuan to Ph. D. candidates.

9. Government of all levels and units will provide high-level talents and returned students with starting fund of scientific projects and essential working conditions. They can also give funds to set up high-tech industry investment service company, provide special loans to key scientific research work, loan guaranty for flowing capital and discounted interests. They aim to expand financing channel and provide effective starting funds for scientific projects by market mechanism.

10. The reform of professional title's system will also be deepened. Inner Mongolia will abort the number restrictions in giving professional titles within scientific institutions. Scientific institutions can decide themselves on the positions and professional ranks they need, and responsibilities and goals of each position will be clarified. Scientific and technical staff can continue their position and treatment during the period of being hired. Scientific institutions can decide the pay according to different positions, tasks and achievements.

11. Subject or academic leaders in institutions of higher learning and scientific experts undertaking great projects and with certain techniques can extend their period of work. Young scientific and technical staff can be promoted according to their achievements, thus creating an environment favorable for talents.

12. Talents are allowed to flow in the need of the market. Technical staff are not restricted by area or ownership of the institutions if they flow within the autonomous region. The institutions getting financial appropriation are not restricted by the authorized size in introducing key technicians, Ph. D.s and talents with great scientific achievements. Professional technicians of institutions of higher learning can undertake the scientific research and operation for enterprises if their own work is not disrupted and the

technological interests of the institutions they are working for not violated.

13. High-level talents can be shared by many institutions. As for high-level professional technicians, they can belong to two or more institutions. Their files will be under the supervision of the Department of Organization of the Inner Mongolia Autonomous Region. Volunteers coming to work in the autonomous region can do part-time, seasonal or flowing work in different regions. Their treatment will be decided by the benefited institutions after consultation with the persons themselves.

14. Institutions should provide money for scientific and technical staff if they want to publish works or articles with important academic scientific value or want to participate in important academic and scientific exchanges with foreign countries. If the institutions have no money, they can apply for help from Talents' Development Fund Management Committee.

15. The health care and housing conditions of high-level talents will be improved. Experts with professional titles of senior rank or enjoying special subsidy from government and young experts with striking contributions will be given medical care cards and assigned regular physical examination and rest. While purchasing the present houses, they will be given a 10 percent reduction in price. High-level talents introduced to work in the region will enjoy the same treatment as the people above. They will be provided housing and transportation tools. Postgraduates and returned students, if work in Inner Mongolia, can be accompanied by their spouses and children, who will enjoy preferential policies in housing, schooling and working. Leagues, cities and institutions should set up apartments for experts to house high-level talents who work for short terms.

16. High-tech enterprises invested and operated by returned overseas students enjoy the same preferential policies as the foreign-funded enterprises. Enterprises of non-public ownership are the same as those of public ownership in introducing professional technicians.

17. (Omitted)

V. Enhance leadership and try to create a favorable condition for talents to play their role.

18. Set up talents' development fund of the autonomous region. This includes the present capital in talents building as well as 5 million yuan appropriated from the autonomous region's finance each year. The fund will be managed a certain department and comprehensively used in training, using and introducing talents. A management committee will be set up by relevant departments and its office will be built in the Department of Personnel of the autonomous region.

19. Party committees and governments at all levels will do a good job of talents training, use and introduction and try to create a favorable condition to respect and protect

talents. Such departments as organization, planning, personnel, labor, science and technology and education will often conduct careful investigations over the talents conditions and study and solve existent problems. The newspapers, radio and TV stations should actively publicize excellent talents making great contributions to the Inner Mongolia. Also, the autonomous region will commend talents and leaders contributing much to the work of the region and relevant departments.

20. Enterprises can follow the above principles in introducing and hiring talents, but they can set up their own conditions.

Appendix IV. Regulations of Inner Mongolia Autonomous Region on Encouraging Taiwan Compatriots Investment (For trial)

Article 1. To enhance the economic and technological exchanges and cooperation between Inner Mongolia Autonomous Region and Taiwan and promote the common prosperity across the Taiwan Straits, Taiwan enterprises and individuals (hereinafter referred to as Taiwan investors) are encouraged to invest in Inner Mongolia. According to the Law of the People's Republic of China on Protecting Taiwan Compatriots Investment and other relevant rules of the state as well as real conditions of the Inner Mongolia, the following regulations are drawn out:

Article 2. Offices of Taiwan Affairs at different levels of people's government are responsible for the organization and coordination of Taiwan compatriots' investment in Inner Mongoila.

Article 3. Taiwan investors are confirmed according to Ways of Identifying Taiwan Investors in Inner Mongolia.

Article 4. Taiwan investors can entrust their relatives or friends as investment agents. The agents must have legal entrustment certificate.

Article 5. Taiwan investors, if want to invest in Inner Mongolia, can select any investment forms unrestricted by relevant laws, regulations and policies of the state and the autonomous region.

Article 6. Taiwan investors are encouraged to invest in the following industries and projects:

(1) Basic industries as infrastructure as energy, transportation, communication and port and important raw materials.

(2) Processing and comprehensive use of farm and animal products, introduction of

new farm and herding technologies and fine breeds and comprehensive development of farm and herding industries, development of green food and proper development and utilization of wild resources.

(3) Productive items with high tee, its running period can be decided by the investors themselves. The running period of joint ventures or cooperative enterprises will be decided on the consultation of all sides concerned.

Article 15. Composition of board of directors and appointment of its chairman in joint ventures and composition of board of directors or joint management institution and appointment of the chairman of the board of directors or director of the joint management institution in cooperative enterprises will be decided by all sides concerned according to their investment proportion or cooperative conditions.

Article 16. If Taiwan investors are to set up joint ventures or cooperative enterprises in Inner Mongolia, the autonomous region side will be responsible for the application. If Taiwan investors are to set up enterprises all of their own, they themselves are responsible for the application, or they can entrust their relatives and friends as well as consulting service agencies in the region to apply for them.

Article 17. Taiwan-invested enterprises, after approval from the customs, can set up bonded plants and bonded storehouses according to law.

Article 18. Taiwan-invested enterprises can hire operation, management staff and employees in or out of China. Relevant departments should help them go through necessary procedures.

Article 19. Taiwan investors or the agents entrusted by them, if they hire their relatives in the enterprises, the relatives can set up household card in the place where the enterprises are and agricultural household registration can be turned into non-agricultural ones.

Article 20. Taiwan-invested enterprises can borrow money from the financial institution of Inner Mongolia with its assets and rights and interests as guaranty.

Article 21. The net profit, dividend, bonus, capital after account settlement and other legal income can be remitted to foreign countries. The salary and other legal incomes of overseas employees hired by the Taiwan-invested enterprises can be remitted or brought to other places than China.

Article 22. Personal property of Taiwan investors and independent operation and management right enjoyed by Taiwan-invested enterprises are protected by law. They cannot be violated by any institution or individual.

Article 23. Taiwan investors can apply for patent and handle other patent affairs and apply for trademark registration and handle other trademark affairs according to law.

Article 24. Except for items stipulated in explicit terms in laws, regulations or by the Inner Mongolian People's Government, no department or institution is allowed to set up other charging lists or raise charging standards in Taiwan-invested enterprises. Examination of Taiwan-invested enterprises must follow rules. Any examination violating the law or state stipulations is forbidden. The enterprises have the right to refuse the training, evaluation, fund collection, donation, exhibition and many other kinds of social activities against their wills.

Article 25. The solely-funded enterprises and shareholding enterprises set up by Taiwan investors enjoy the following preferential policies as well as those stipulated by the laws, regulations and policies at the state or autonomous region levels.

(1) Priorities will be given to Taiwan-invested enterprises in the use of land, water, electricity, transportation and communication facilities. Banks will give them loans first if they need productive or operational funds. They will be given priority in getting production and operation permission certificates. As for some special items, special preferential policies will be given.

(2) As for productive enterprises having run for more than 10 years, if they are engaged in items encouraged by the autonomous region, the enterprise income tax in the first five years after profit-making will be refunded after examination by local finance and taxation departments, and the 25 percent of the value added tax (VAT) previously kept by local finance department will also be refunded. The Taiwan-invested productive enterprises in Hohhot, frontier banners and cities and high-tech development zones with an operation period of more than 10 years will enjoy relevant preferential policies in taxation in these areas. However, if an enterprise does not run for 10 years as expected, the refunded income tax and VAT should be recovered.

(3) Taiwan investors in poverty-stricken areas at the state or autonomous region levels and frontier banners and counties will be exempted from urban real estate tax in the first five years. The license tax of motor vehicles or boats and tax of using urban land will be levied but will be refunded five years later.

(4) Taiwan solely-invested or shareholding enterprises will pay for the land use right, which will be refunded later. In five years staring from operation, the proportion kept by local finance department will be fully refunded.

Article 26. Taiwan investors, if use their profits gained from enterprises in Inner Mongolia to reinvest in the same enterprises or new enterprises and with an operation period of no less than five years, shall be refunded 40 percent of the business income taxes in the reinvestment. If their reinvestment goes to export-oriented enterprises or high-tech enterprises, all the paid business income taxes shall be refunded.

Article 27. The Taiwan-invested productive items involving an investment of US$10 million or above enjoy all preferential policies of the economic and technological development zone of the autonomous region.

Article 28. Taiwan investors enjoy relevant policies of the autonomous region in revitalizing small state-owned enterprises if they participate in the reform, reorganization and reform of medium-sized and small industries and enterprises at the autonomous region, league or city levels. Taiwan investors can purchase competitive state-owned enterprises according to law, or participate in the auction of bankrupted enterprises.

Article 29. Taiwan investors should come to and go out of Inner Mongolia with Pass of Taiwan Residents to and from China's Mainland and other valid certificates. If they need to go between the two places, they can be given signature for many times upon application and approval and given temporary residence certificate.

Article 30. Taiwan-invested enterprises enjoy the same treatment as to local state-owned enterprises in purchasing machinery equipment, raw materials and auxiliary materials and using water, electricity, heat, cargo transportation, labor, advertisement, communication and telephone installation.

Article 31. Taiwan investors and accompanying relatives and Taiwan employees hired by Taiwan-invested enterprises enjoy the same treatment as local residents in asking for temporary residential certificates as well as in purchasing houses, lodging, medical care, transportation and communications.

Article 32. Children of Taiwan investors and Taiwan employees in Taiwan-invested enterprises have priority in going to middle and primary schools in Inner Mongolia.

Article 33. Taiwan investors, their family members and employees with driving license or temporary driving license outside China can be directly given driving license or temporary driving license of Inner Mongolia.

Article 34. The People's Government of Inner Mongolia Autonomous Region sets up agencies to receive complaints from Taiwan investors. The Taiwan investors can also submit their complaints to relevant administrative and judicial departments by themselves. The relevant administrative and judicial departments should handle cases involving violation of the body and property interests of Taiwan investors in time, carefully investigate them and give fair conclusions according to law.

Article 35. Intermediaries who introduce Taiwan investors to Inner Mongolia will be awarded according to relevant regulations of the autonomous region government.

Article 36. The regulations shall come into effect from the date of their promulgation. The right to interpret these regulations resides in the Office of Opening-up Affairs of the Inner Mongolia Autonomous Region.

Appendix V. Economic and Technological Development Zones

Name: Baotou Rare Earth New and High-Tech Industrial Development Zone

Address: Rare Earth Development Zone, South Qinggong Road, Qingshan District, Baotou

Zip: 014030   Area code: 0472   Fax: 5156391

Business Invitation Bureau: 5159784   Innovation center: 5154670

Name: Manzhouli Frontier Economic Cooperative Area

Address: Building of the Economic Cooperation Management Committee, East Wuda Street, Manzhouli

Zip: 021400   Area code: 0470   Fax: 6220344

Business Invitation Bureau: 6234707   Audit Bureau: 6225165

Name: Erenhot Frontier Economic Cooperative Area

Address: Second floor of the Lianjian Building, North Youyi Road, Erenhot

Zip: 011100   Area code: 0479

Fax: 7521164 (Extension)   Office: 7523512

Name: Management Committee of Hohhot Ruyi Economic and Technological Development Zone

Address: No. 1 Yiwei Road, Ruyi Economic and Technological Development Zone, Hohhot

Zip: 010010   Area code: 0471   Fax: 4929877

Name: Management Committee of Jinchuan Resources Economic and Technological Development Zone

Address: No. 1 Jinhai Road, Jinchuan Economic and Technological Development Zone, Hohhot

Zip: 010080   Area code: 0471   Fax: 3901211

Policies and Legal Affairs Office: 3901239

Name: Management Committee of Hailar Economic and Technological Development Zone

Address: Shangcheng East Road, Hailar Economic and Technological Development Zone

Zip: 021000   Area code: 0470   Fax: 8350174

Office: 8350861

Name: Management Committee of Tongliao Development Zone

Address: Heping Road, Tongliao
Zip: 280002   Area code: 0475   Fax: 8238407
Name: Chifeng Pingzhuang Economic and Technological Development Zone
Address: North Ring Road of Pingzhuang, Chifeng
Zip: 024076   Area code: 0476   Fax: 3511757
Comprehensive Office: 3517960   Coordinating Office: 3512415
Name: Chifeng Qiaoxi Economic and Technological Development Zone
Address: Qiaoxi District of Chifeng
Zip: 024005   Area code: 0476   Fax: 8449277
Office: 8440885   Liaison Office: 8440885
Name: Chifeng Hongshan Comprehensive Development Experimental Area
Address: Government of Hongshan District
Zip: 024000   Area code: 0476   Fax: 8240060
Name: Arxan Development Zone
Address: Arxan Development Zone
Zip: 137800   Area code: 0482   Fax: 8822374
Name: Management Committee of Linhe Economic and Technological
Development Zone
Address: West to the West Ring Road, Linhe
Zip: 015000   Area code: 0478   Fax: 8218323
Name: Management Committee of Wulagai Development Zone
Address: Management Committee of Wulagai Development Zone
Zip: 026300   Area code: 0479   Fax: 3351373
Name: Management Committee of Hangjin Agriculture Economic and
Technological Development Zone
Address: Hangjin Agriculture Economic and Technological Development Zone
Zip: 017400   Area code: 0477   Fax: 6623362
Name: Manzhouli East Lake Export and Foreign Currency-Oriented
Agricultural Development Zone
Zip: 021400   Area code: 0470   Fax: 6541034
Administrative Bureau: 6541034
Name: Junggar Shagedu Economic and Technological Development Zone
Address: Junggar Shagedu Economic and Technological Development Zone
Zip: 017100   Area code: 0477   Fax: 4925160
Office: 4925160, 4925181   Business Invitation Bureau: 4925284

Appendix VI. Address Book of Offices of Inner Mongolia Autonomous Region Stationed in other cities

Beijing Office

No. 47 Chongwenmennei Street, Dongcheng District, Beijing

Telephone exchange: 65242131 Area code: 010   Zip: 100005

Fax: 65136517   Line on duty: 64014499-8218

Comprehensive Sector: 65137696 3112

Economic Information Sector: 65131144 (Labor affairs) 3103, 3104

Reception Sector: 64014499-8218, 3101

Financial Room: 65131382, 3113

Dongdan Hotel: 65131383, 3106, 3109

Commercial Center: 65131143, 3115   65136517 (Fax)

Office of Basic Construction: 65243921-3111

Menglian Company: 3118, 3119

Shenzhen Office

The 28th Floor of the East Wing of the International Trade Center, South Renmin Road, Shenzhen

Area code: 0755   Fax: 2273303   Zip: 518046

Line on duty: 2242677

Shanghai Office

The 16th Floor of the Lianhe Building, No. 2650 North Zhongshan Road, Shanghai

Fax: 62577622   Area code: 021   Zip: 200063

Office: 62577341   62165719

Tianjin Office

No. 14 Sanjing Road, Hebei District, Tianjin

Telephone exchange: 24464265

Area code: 022   Zip: 300010   Fax: 24467617

Line on duty: 24464265-8808

Comprehensive Office: 24464265-8868

Shenyang Office

4-1-3, No. 3 of Lane 49, Shifu Avenue, Heping District, Shenyang

Area code: 024

Zip: 110001   Office: 23831530   Company: 23831551

Shenzhen Office

The 28th Floor of the East Wing of the International Trade Center, South Renmin

Road, Shenzhen

    Area code: 0755   Fax: 2273303   Zip: 518046

    Line on duty: 2242677

Guangzhou Office

No. 2 West Lane 2, Zhijie Street, Jingtai New Village, Guangyuan Road, Guangzhou

Telephone exchange: 86590469

Area code: 020

Zip: 510405

Fax: 86596705

Line on duty: 86590469-2100

Office: 2202

Business invitation Office: 2202

Harbin Office

No. 76 Hetu Street, Daoli District, Harbin

Telephone exchange: 4603301, 4603302

Area code: 0451   Line on duty: 4603301-8101

Zip: 150076   Reception: 8202   Hainan Office: 6253223

Wuhan Office

2807161, 1394711075

Qinhuangdao Office:

3034985 3030050   3036263   3036135   3036262   3036232

Xiamen Office:

The 5th floor, No. 490 Changqing Road, Xiamen

Zip: 361012   Fax: 5072449   Tel: 5150168 (0592)

Appendix VII. Major Scenic Spots and Tour Routes in Inner Mongolia Autonomous Region

1. State-level tour routes and scenic spots

(1) Beijing--Hohhot (Tomb of Wang Zhaojun, Wuta Temple, Dazhao Monastery, Xilitu Monastery, White Tower, Inner Mongolia Museum, Mosque) --Grassland (in Xilamuren or Gegentala)

(2) Beijing--Hohhot (city and grassland visits) -Baotou (Wudang Monastery) -Dalad Banner of Ih Ju (Xiangshawan, or Sand Singing Bay) -Hohhot-Beijing

(3) Beijing-Hohhot (city and grassland visits)--Dalad Banner of Ih Ju (Xiangshawan, or Sand Singing Bay) -Dongshen (cashmere plant) -Mausoleum of Genghis Khan

(including his resort) --Hohhot-Beijing

(4) Beijing or Hohhot-Hailar (Western Hill Pine Forest Park, Erqi Underground Defense Works, Museum of Ethnic Groups, Folk art crafts plant) -Chen Barag Banner (Hoh Nur Grassland) or Ewenki Autonomous Banner (Bayan Huxu Grassland) -Hailar-Beijing

(5) Beijing or Hohhot-Hailar (city tour) -Manzhouli (Dalai Lake, Xiaohekou, grassland, gateway, Sino-Russian trading area) -Hailar-Beijing

2. Autonomous Region-level tour routes and scenic spots

(1) Beijing-Hohhot (Tomb of Wang Zhaojun, Wuta Temple, Dazhao Monastery, Xilitu Monastery, White Tower, Inner Mongolia Museum, Mosque, Nationality Articles Plant) --Grasslands (in Xilamuren, Gegentala or Huitengxile) -Hohhot-Beijing

(2) Beijing-Hohhot (city tour) -Hasuhai (Hasuhai Tourism and Holiday Village) - Baotou (through Meidai Monastery, Wudang Monastery, Saihantala Tourism and Holiday Village, Zhaojun Island, Palace of the Journey to the West, Baotou Cashmere Plant, Baotou Iron and Steel Plant) -Urad Front Banner (Ulansuhai Holiday Center) or-Dalad Banner of Ih Ju League (Engebei Desert, Xiangshawan) -Dongsheng (cashmere plant, Yuandai Village) -Mausoleum of Genghis Khan (including his resort) -Hohhot-Beijing

(3) Hohhot or Beijing-Xilin Hot (Golden Top Tent, Qagan Obo, Beizi Temple, Nationality Articles Plant, Carpet Plant) -Xiritala (grassland tourism and holiday center) or Zhenglan Banner (typical pastoral scenery, flat top hill, sandy area scene, Summer Palace of Kublai Khan, Shangdu Ruins of the Yuan Dynasty, Jinlianchuan) -Xilin Hot-Beijing

(4) Beijing-Chengde-Ningcheng (hot water spring, Daming Pagoda, forest area of Xidaogou along the Heili River, Falun Temple, Ningcheng Liquor Plant) -Harqin (Lingyue and Longquan temples) -Chifeng (Hongshan Cultural Museum, Hongshan National Forest Park, Red Star Sculpture Plant) -Ongniud Banner (Qigan Grassland, desert and tourism area of folk customs) --Hexigten Banner (Huanggang Fruit Forest Field, Dali Lake Tourism and Holiday Area, Ulan Butong) -Mulan hunting ground-Chengde

(5) Shenyang-Hure Banner (Ancient Temple Group) -Daqinggou (forest nature reserve) -Tongliao (city tour, Jirem League Museum, Cruising on the Molimiaosha Lake by pleasure boat or motor boat) -Jurh River Grassland Tourism Area-Tongliao-Beijing

(6) Beijing or Changchun-Ulan Hot (Temple of Genghis Khan, site of the "May Day" Meeting-Cha'ersen Reservoir (Cha'ersen Mongolian yurt tourism village)

(7) Hohhot or Beijing-Hailar (city tour) -Chen Barag Banner (Hoh Nur Pastoral Tour) or Ewenki Autonomous Banner (Bayan Huxu Pastoral Tour) -Manzhouli (Dalai

Lake, national gateway, Sino-Russian trading fair) -Jalai Nur (Fossil of mammoth) -Shamiaogou (pastoral scene, fishing on the Hulun Lake) -Manzhouli-Harbin

(8) Hailar (city tour) -Yakeshi (Phoenix Villa, watching the sun rise in the sea of forest, finishing at the Zhadun River) -Zhalantun (Xiushui Park, suspended bridge) -Qiqihar or Beijing

(9) Hohhot-Erenhot (national gateway, Sino-Mongolian trading fair, Erenhot Dinosaur Ruins, Dinosaur Museum) -Siziwang Banner (Gegentala Pastoral Tour) -Hohhot (city tour)

(10) Beijing or Hohhot (city tour) -Yinchuan (Mausoleum of Western Xia Kings, Sandy Lake, Western Film City) -Bayan Hot of Arxan League (grassland made by aerial sowing, Yanfu Temple, North Temple, climbing Helan Mountains) -Ejina Banner-Heicheng Ruins-Yinchuan

(11) Hohhot (city tour) -Liangcheng (Daihai, sightseeing Daihai on boats, fishing, swimming, Manhanshan National Forest Park, Memorial Hall of the Revolutionary Ruins of He Long) -Hohhot

Appendix VIII. Special Tour Routes of Inner Mongolia

1. Hailar Ice and Snow Tour

Beijing-Hailar-Chen Barag Banner (Hohhot Pastoral Tour) or Ewenki Autonomous Banner (Bayan Huxu Pastoral Tour)

2. Horse Tour

(1) Beijing-Hohhot-Siziwang Banner-Gegentala-Wangfu No. 2 Team-Qagan Obo-Amgalang-Jiang'an Herding Field-Habuqi-Damiao-Gegentala-Hohhot-Beijing

(2) Beijing-Hohhot-Xilamuren Grassland-Bailing Temple-Hohhot-Beijing

(3) Beijing-Hohhot-Xilin Hot-Bayin Xile Herding Field-Mati (Horse Hoof) Mountain-Dali Lake-Xilin Hot

3. Bicycle Tour

(1) Beijing-Hohhot-Siziwang Banner Gegentala Grassland-Xilamuren-Wudang Monastery-Guyang-Xiangshawan-Dongsheng-Mausoleum of Genghis Khan-Junggar Banner-Xuejiawan-Hohhot-Beijing

(2) Beijing-Hailar-Mudamoji-Xinkai Lake-Dalai Lake-Xiaohekou-Manzhouli-Back Baikal-Manzhouli-Hoh Nur-Hailar-Beijing

4. Motorcycle Tour

(1) Beijing-Hohhot-Xilamuren Grassland-Bailing Temple-Guyang-Baotou-

Dongsheng-Junggar--Tuoxian-Hohhot-Beijing

(2) Beijing-Hohhot-Siziwang Banner-Gegentala Grassland-Saihantala of Xilin Gol League-Erenhot-Xilin Hot-Zhenglan Banner-Zhangjiakou-Beijing

5. Automobile Tour

(1) Beijing-Hohhot-Saihantala-Erenhot-Xilin Hot-West Ujimqin Banner-Linxi-Keshiketeng Banner-Chifeng-Ningcheng hot water-Chengde-Beijing

(2) Beijing-Baotou-Mausoleum of Genghis Khan-Yan'an-Xi'an

6. Nomadic Tour

(1) Beijing-Xilin Hot-Xiritala Grassland-West Ujimqin Banner （lodging in herdsmen's houses, learning to make milk products, experiencing herdsmen's life, grazing sheep, putting up Mongolian yurts）

(2) Beijing-Hailar-Chen Barag Banner Bayin Had-East Wuzhuer--West Wuzhuer--Chagang-Xiaohekou-Manzhouli-Hailar-Beijing

7. Exploration Tour in Badain Jaran

Beijing-Hohhot （or Yinchuan） -Bayan Hot-Alxa Right Banner-Badain Jaran Desert （walking through it or going through it by camels）

8. Warm Spring Tour of Arxan

Beijing-Ulan Hot-Arxan-Baichengzi-Beijing

9. Forest Tour of Hulun Buir

Hailar-Yakeshi （Phoenix Villa） -Genhe （Forest Tourism and Holiday Village） -Oroqen Autonomous Banner-Hailar

10. Archaeology Tour

Chifeng-Ningcheng-Bairin Right Banner-Bairin Left Banner-Chifeng

11. Grassland Summer Camp

Beijing-Hohhot-Gegentala Grassland of Siziwang Banner （Opening ceremony, speech by headmaster, setting up Mongolian yurts, picnic, lectures, watching sunrise on grassland, setting up stoves to make dishes, climbing Aobao mountains, visiting herdsmen, campfire party, collecting plant specimens, cooking dishes, graduation ceremony, issuing graduation certificates） -Hohhot--Beijing

Postscript

It is a great decision made by China to implement the strategy of western development and accelerate the development of central and western China facing the new century. The western development has aroused wide concern from home and abroad. As China is soon to join the World Trade Organization, the multilateral opening-up in the country will step onto a new stage. The western development also provides unprecedented cooperation and development opportunities to people both from other places of China and foreign countries. As one of the provinces and autonomous regions in western region and the first minority autonomous region of China, Inner Mongolia is specially concentrated. Now we present this book Western China-Inner Mongolia Autonomous Region to the world, hoping that readers can fully understand the short-term and long-term development plans of the autonomous region as well as many of its preferential policies, thus enhancing the exchanges and cooperation between Inner Mongolia and countries and regions of the world and deepening the understanding and friendship between peoples.

After more than 50 years of construction, Inner Mongolia has seen earth-shaking changes in all aspects of social lives. The spring breeze of China's reform and opening-up has inserted wings to the autonomous region. Now Inner Mongolia enjoys social stability, economic development, national unity and peaceful life. Each aspect shows that it is stepping toward improvement, civilization and modernization. The 50 years development and progress of Inner Mongolia has provided precious experiences to the whole country in regional national autonomy, properly solving national contradictions and problems and greatly promoting the economic and social development in frontier and minority ethnic group areas.

Though great development and progress has been made, Inner Mongolia is left far behind compared with developed eastern areas. The 23 million people of all ethnic groups in Inner Mongolia will abide by the Deng Xiaoping Theory and basic routes of the CPC and follow the basic principles of "grasping opportunity, deepening reform, expanding opening-up, promoting development and maintaining stability". Taking the historic opportunity of western development, they will promote the comprehensive economic strength, sustainable development ability and people's quality of the region.

Taking advantage of its significant position in western development and in accordance with the five focuses determined by the state and five strategies put forward by Inner Mongolia, it will build itself into the most important ecological defense line in north China and develop three areas of different functions. It will also finish 10 projects and three goals. The final aim is to turn Inner Mongolia into an economic growth point of China in the 21st century. On the basis of present preferential policies, Inner Mongolia is now actively studying new policies and measures for deepening reform and expanding opening-up so as to attract more talents, capital and technology to the development and construction of the autonomous region. Its final aim is to set up a "policy basin" to attract all kinds of production factors, thereby creating a favorable investment environment for western development.

Information Office of Inner Mongolia People's Government

January 2001